ORDERLY BOOKS OF THE REVOLUTION,

NO. 2.

VIEW OF A PART OF THE MOORE HOUSE, IN NEWTOWN,
LONG ISLAND, N.Y.

This part, where this book was found, now used as a dining-room,
was built by John Moore, about 1660, and is still
in the possession of the family.

ORDERLY BOOK

OF THE

"MARYLAND LOYALISTS REGIMENT,"

JUNE 18th, 1778, to OCTOBER 12th, 1778.

INCLUDING GENERAL ORDERS ISSUED BY SIR HENRY CLINTON, BARON WILHELM VON KUYPHAUSEN, SIR WILLIAM ERSKINE, CHARLES, LORD CORNWALLIS, GENERAL WILLIAM TRYON AND GENERAL OLIVER DE LANCEY.

KEPT BY

CAPTAIN CALEB JONES.

———

EDITED BY

PAUL LEICESTER FORD.

———

CLEARFIELD

Originally published
Brooklyn, New York, 1891

Reprinted for
Clearfield Company, Inc. by
Genealogical Publishing Co., Inc.
Baltimore, Maryland
1996

International Standard Book Number: 0-8063-4645-0

Made in the United States of America

NOTE.

SINCE the foregoing history of this regiment was printed, I have discovered that it was transferred to Florida in 1779, or the early part of 1780. At the surrender of the English force at Mobile to Don Bernardo de Galvez, March 14, 1780, among the prisoners taken were "Of the Maryland corps.—1 Sergeant, 15 rank and file."* Not quite a year later, on May 9, 1781, a much larger part were made prisoners of war by Gen. Campbell's surrender of Pensacola to the Spaniards; described in the "state of the forces composing the Garrison of Fort St. George" as "Maryland Loyalists, 1 Major, 4 Captains, 2 first Lieutenants, 5 Ensigns Staff; 1 quarter master, 1 mate. Serjeants, &c. 9 serjeants, 8 corporals, 3 drummers and fifers, 101 privates. Wounded 1 private. Sick and invalid; 1 serjeant."† In "Farmers Journal of the Siege of Pensacola,"‡ are a few facts concerning the part borne by this regiment, Major M'Donald being at that time the officer in command. From this same source we learn that the prisoners were transferred to Havana, and on June 30, 1781, sailed for New York, where they arrived on July 12, and were cantoned in and about Newtown, L. I.

---

* Almon's Remembrancer, 1780, II, 99.

† Almon's Remembrancer, 1782, II, 281.

‡ Historical Magazine, IV, 166.

INTRODUCTION.

THE greatest problem of the British government, in their attempt to subdue the rebellion of the United Colonies, was the difficulty of obtaining soldiers. From early times, the superior condition of the British subject had made him loth to serve his country either in the navy or army. The former difficulty had been overcome by the impressment laws, which, limited in their effect to the seaport towns and directed largely against non-residents and criminals, produced only passing ebullitions of discontent. To fill the ranks of the latter, however, no administration had dared to risk the unpopularity of a conscription law, and in her wars Great Britain had for many years relied quite as much on a subsidy system for procuring allies and armies, as upon her own troops. On the breaking out of the American Revolution, this problem offered greater difficulties than usual. Not only was the war one which did not inspire national enthusiasm, but a large per centage of the people and the Opposition in Parliament believed it to be unjust; and the general ignoranceof the people of Great Britain of America, as well as its great distance, all combined to make recruiting a failure in the mother-country. Convinced

of

of this inability to obtain the necessary quotas at home, the Ministry sought aid outside. The Hessians oɪ Germany and the Indians of Canada were obtained— troops so cruel as to actually preclude the possibility of conciliation — and from the Colonies themselves were drawn still another force — "the Loyalists" — who, embittered by past persecution, and by the fratricidal nature of the contest, proved scarcely less merciless and vindictive.

Upon the evacuation of Boston, a corps of the refugees from that city was embodied under the command of Timothy Ruggles. After the occupation of New York and the overrunning of New Jersey, the New York Loyalists were organized into De Lancey's Brigade, and New Jersey supplied the troops for Skinner's New Jersey Volunteers, making a force computed in May, 1777, to number about two thousand men. In this year General Howe carried the main part of his army from the head of the Elk, in Chesapeake Bay, through or near the strongly loyal Colonies of Maryland and Delaware, and occupied Philadelphia. This city had an estimated population of some twenty thousand who were neutral or loyal to the King's rule, and large bodies of loyalists in the march had taken the opportunity to join the English forces. Upon taking possession of that city, therefore, further attempts were made to enlist loyalist corps, and among others, Sir William Howe gave permission to James Chalmers, "a gentleman from Maryland, who came into

into the British Army at Elk;"* "much respected in the three Lower Counties on Delaware and in Maryland,"† to raise a regiment to be known as the "Maryland Loyalists." ‡ This act was afterwards criticised by an opponent of Howe on the ground that Chalmers, "though much respected in Maryland, was unconnected and without influence in Philadelphia;" ‖ but his regiment met with as much success in recruiting as any of the loyalists, and so far as we can judge from the names of the officers, was drawn entirely from Maryland; though by General Robertson's evidence the rank and file of most of the loyal regiments were composed of newly-arrived emigrants. In May, 1778, Chalmers' regiment was stated to number 336 in all, and it is probable that, cut off from its recruiting base by the evacuation of Philadelphia in the next month, it never numbered more. A partial roster of the regiment is here given. For the commission officers it is believed to be complete :¶

---

* Galloway's *Examination*, 67.

† Howe's *Evidence*, 53.

‡ In Montressor's Journal it was also called "the 3d Provincial Regt.' In the New York Historical Society's copy of Rivington's *Army List* for 1783 a MS. note records that the uniform was "Red Coat, Olive lapel white button holes."

‖ Galloway's *Examination*, 67.

¶ The numbers following the names indicate the works they are given in, as follows: No. 1, this Orderly Book; No. 2, Mills & Hicks' *Register* for 1779; No. 3, Gaines' *Register* for 1781; No. 4, Gaines' *Register* for 1782; No. 5, Sabine's *American* Loyalists. No. 6. Rivington's *Army list* 1783.

James

James Chalmers, Lieutenant Colonel, 1, 2, 3, 4, 5, 6.

James McDonald, Major, 1, 2, 3.

Captains.

Grafton Dulany, 1, 2, 3, 6.

Caleb Jones, 1, 2, 3, 4, 5, 6.

Philip Barton Key,* 1, 2, 3, 4, 5, 6.

Isaac Costen,† 1, 2, 3, 4, 5.

Patrick Kennedy, 1, 2, 3, 4, 5.

Walter Dulaney,‡ 1, 2.

James Frisby, 1, 2, 3, 4.

Daniel Dulaney Addison,§ 4, 5, 6.

Lieutenants.

James Miller,‖ 2, 3.

James Sinclair, 1, 2.

John Stirling, 2, 4, 5, 6.

John Boswell, 2.

James Inglis, 1, 2, 3, 5.

Thomas H. Parker, 1, 2, 3.

Levin Townsend, 1, 2, 3, 4, 6.

Ensigns.

William Stirling, 1, 2, 3, 4, 6.

William Bowles, 1, 2, 4, 6.

James Henley,¶ 2, 3, 4, 5, 6.

John Coffman, 2, 3, 4.

John Stewart, 4, 6.

Winder Cannon, 1, 2, 3.

William Jones, 1, 2, 3.

William Monro, 1, 2, 3, 4.

John McPherson, 1.

John Patterson, Chaplain, 2, 3, 5.

Surgeons.

———— Kidd, 2.

———— Stafford, 5.

---

* In Gaines' *Register* for 1781 he is entered as Phillip R. Key, but in the issue for 1782, as above.

† *Sabine* gives the name Costin (II, 500).

‡ In Gaines' *Register* for 1782 he is Major, in place of McDonald.

§ *Sabine* gives it "Daniel Delany Addison."

‖ Spelt in Gaines' *Register* for 1781 "Millar." In that year he was Adjutant.

¶ In 1782 he was Adjutant, Gaines' *Register*.

† In Rivington's *Army list* it is spelled Stuart.

Quarter

Quarter Masters.

Joseph Gaeuelt, 2.	Thomas Welch, 4, 6.
William Stafford, Mate, 2.	William Heuston, Mate, 2, 4.

Sergeants.

Zachariah Bailey, 1.	James Love, 1.
Joshua Merrill, 1.	——— Dimant, 1.
Thomas Gill, 1.	——— More, 1.
——— Stratton, 1.	

Corporals.

Obediah Smith, 1.	John White, 1.
Jacob Rodger, 1.	

Peter Brown, Private, 1.

The Maryland Loyalists remained in Philadelphia until the beginning of its evacuation, June 16, 1778. It crossed New Jersey with the remainder of Howe's army, being part of General Knyphausen's division, taking part in the battle of Monmouth, and upon its arrival at Sandy Hook was transferred to Long Island, and attached to the command of General Tryon. In this service they occupied different posts on the island, largely for the purpose of procuring fresh provisions and forage. From England, with the probabilities, in those days, of a six to ten weeks' voyage, only salt provisions were obtainable, and the English army was even at times on short allowance of these. To supply the commissariat was therefore a constant struggle, which led to much that disgraced and made the English hated beyond description. So disagreeable was this service to the regular force, that it was largely left to the Hessians and Loyalists, who, trained to see whatever

ever was needed being taken by force (or as it was delicately veiled by words, "impressed"), and having neither patriotism or *corps d'ésprit* to check them, plundered and destroyed at their own pleasure. Of all parts of the Colonies, Long Island probably suffered the most. Occupied by the British from 1776 to 1783, it was depended on for a large part of these supplies, but which the policy of the United Colonies was to destroy. It was therefore the scene of constant descents, skirmishing and harrying, in which the inhabitants were as the nut between the crackers; and these have left a story of brutality and destruction hardly to be equalled, which finds narration in all of our town and county histories. These so shamed the finer feelings of the leaders of the British army that they not merely condemned the few ever convicted, but in at least one case paid out of their own pocket for the destruction done; but the people for the most part dared make no complaint, and indeed both Howe and the Continental Congress complained that for the worst crime committed, but few could be brought to acknowledge its committal. In this occupation the Maryland Loyalists passed the summer and early fall of 1778, and seem to have continued near or in New York till 1782, in which year they served in Florida. A year later, on the conclusion of peace, the larger part of them embarked at New York, on the transport ship *Martha*, for Nova Scotia, to settle there, but were wrecked off Tusket river, and over one hundred lives

lives lost. It is recorded that the troops stood, drawn up in company order, while the women and children were ordered into the boats, and the few survivors among the men were chiefly saved by clinging to wreckage.

The orderly book of this regiment, here printed, covers the period from June 18, 1778, to October 12, 1778. It begins with the evacuation of Philadelphia, and covers the march across the Jerseys, and the foraging tour and cantonment on Long Island. For the period to July 5th, the General Orders of Howe have been printed in the "Kemble Papers," in the *Collections of the New York Historical Society for 1882;* but there are differences in the following text even in these, and this includes as well the Brigade and Regimental Orders, which were of course not included in the General Orders. For the remainder of the period it fills a gap which has hitherto been vacant, making it of great importance historically. It is also, so far as I can ascertain, the first orderly book of the Loyalists put in print, and has a value, both to the genealogist and to the Maryland historian, who has even failed as yet to mention this regiment. It was kept by Caleb Jones, once sheriff of Somerset county, in Maryland, who in 1776 was arrested and only set at liberty by the Council of Safety on his giving bonds for £200 for his obedience to the self-constituted Whig authorities. He seems to have sought safety in Lord Dunmore's fleet, for he arrived at New York in the frigate *Brune*
a few

a few months later, and for this flight the General Court at Annapolis declared him an outlaw. He went with the English army to Philadelphia, where he enlisted in the Maryland Loyalists with the rank of captain. At the conclusion of the peace he removed to St. John's, New Brunswick, being one of the original grantees of that city.

This Orderly Book was left in the garret of the John Moore house, at Newtown, having been presumably tossed aside when filled up, for the regiment was then in quarters there. Here it was discovered by Mr. Oliver Hazard Perry, the occupant, whose wife Maria Louisa Moore is a descendant of John Moore, the builder of the house.

PAUL LEICESTER FORD.

97 Clark St., Brooklyn, N. Y.

ORDERLY BOOK.

Parole, *Jersey.*   C. Sign, *Brunswick.*

The Commander in Chief [Sir Henry Clinton] Expects That the Commanding Officers will strictly inforce all Orders Relative to Disapline and Good Orders, and it being the Gen^ls Intention to have the Army as amply Supplyd as the situation will or can Submitt of—He Desires that it may be Understood that he is fully Determined to Execute in the spott Every Man Deticted in Mauroding or who Shall Quitt his poast, Upon the March, or found straglin by the Advance poasts of the Corp without permition; all Persons who have permition to follow the Armey are immediately to Give in their Names to the Late Town Magor [Capt. Edward Madden] of Philadelphia, Shoughing Their Names by whome Recommended—

---

* On June 16, Howe ordered "Lieutenant-Gen. Knyphausen and Maj.-Gen. Grant [to] cross the River to-morrow morning at four with the following Corps (viz.) Yagers' mounted and Dismouted, Queen's Rangers, Hessian Grenadiers, 2d New Jersey Volunteers, Maryland Loyalists, Volunteers of Ireland, and Caledonian Volunteers." That day's march brought them to Haddonfield, about eight miles from Philadelphia, on the Gloucester and Moorestown turnpike.

A Return

A Return of wemin Actually with Each Corps to be Given in to Morrow at Orderly Time. The women of the army are Constantly to March on the flanks of the Baggage of thier Respective Corps, and the provost Marshal had Received Possitive Orders to Drum out Every Woman who shall Dear to Disobay this Order. The Commanding Officers of Corps will at all Times, when they Cume to their Ground, post such Guards and Pickets as they shall judge sufficient for the safety of their Incampments—The Pickets of Each Brigade of Brittish are to be Visited by a field Officer Belongin to it; he is to Report al Extreordenareys to the Coll of the Day for the Infermation of the Commander in Chief, and His Excellency Gen¹ Kniphousin* will Please to Order such Officer as he shall think Proper to Vissit the poasts of The Heation Troops under his Command. The Gen¹ Orders of the Army will be Given at 6 O'Clock In the Morning Untill further Orders.

For the Day to Morrow [Coll Lieut.] [West] Hyde —M[ajor] B[rigade].—Syms.†

HEAD-QUARˢ, HADDENFIELD, JUNE Yᴱ 19th, 1778.

Parole, *Amboy*.　　　　C. Sign, *New York*.

Gen¹ Kniphousens Orders—

The Troops to hold them Selves in Readiness to

---

* Baron Wilhelm von Knyphausen, the commander of the Hessians.

† Probably Lieut. James Symes.

March

March on the Shortest Notice—The Adj^t to attend this Night for Orders at Genl. Grants* at 8 O'Clock· The Armey to Move to Morrow Morning at 2 OClock to march of from the Right by half Divitions when Ever the Road will Permitt it. The advance g^d to Consist of ye 4 and 15th Reg^t to the Detatchmt ye 16th Dragoons—The British Infintrey ye 28th Regt 49th – 23^d – 27th – 55th and 15th Regements, Teams & Vallentear Baggage shall of Pionears of Colo. Chalmers† Corps—and jarsey Vollinteers Baggage of the Genl Officers Teams of Artillerys Baggage of the Army According to the Order of March. The Remainders of the Pionears and provision Train Pontoons ye 10th Reg^t with Coll. Chalmers and jersey Vollinteers‡ to flank the Baggage Artillery and provition Train They all to be Equally Devided and be attentive That no stragler Commit this Order for which they will Responsibly. One Hession Regt. and 5th British to Compose the Rare guard. One Officer and party of The 17th Dragoons to Clear the whole. The Flanking Parteys of the Collums to Continew Till This County Appear open.

---

* Major General James Grant, commanding the second division.

† Lieutenant Colonel James Chalmers, commissioned Oct. 14, 1777, commander of the "Maryland Loyalists." A sketch of him is given in *Sabine.*

‡ Gen. Courtland Skinner's "New Jersey Volunteers." Cf. Stryker's *The New Jersey Volunteers*, Trenton, 1887.

HEAD QUARS MORES TOWN [Moorestown, N. J.*]
JUNE 20th

Parole, *Prauge*.　　　　　C. Sign, *Colingin*.

The Army to March to morrow Morning at 3
OClock from The Right in the same Order as to Day
—The 28th Rigt. to form the advance Guard followed
by the Detachment of the 17th Dragoons of which a
Corpl. and 6 to March in front of the 28th. The 10th
Regt. and Coll Chalmers Corps and The Jersey Vol-
linteers to flank the Baggage Artilrey and provition
Train—The Rear guard Donops Regt. and ye 5th
British Followed by the Detatchment of ye 17th Dra-
goons—

A Copy of sir Henrey Clinton's Order. Camp at
Evening [?]† Times 19th June 1778.

The Right honnerable [Capt. Francis] Lord Raw-
don is Oppoynted Adjt. Genl. With the Rank of
Lieut. Collonell in the Armey in the Room of Lt.
Collo. [James] Patterson who has omitted‡ Leave to
Return to Europe on his private affairs.

---

*About seven miles northeast of Haddonfield.

† In the order as printed in the *Kemble Papers* (1, 595) it is " Ever-
sham," but the word here used is certainly not that.

‡ "Obtained" in *Kemble Papers* (1, 595).

HEAD QUAR<u>S</u>. MOUNT HOLLY JUNE YE 20TH 78.

All Orders Delivered by Cap<u>t</u> [Thomas] Murr[a]y
of the 40<u>th</u> * Reg<u>t</u> or Cap<u>t</u> [John] L[l]oyd of the 46<u>th</u>
Regt. are to be Obayed as Coming from an Adee-
camp.

———————

HEAD QUAR<u>S</u>. MOUNT HOLLEY JUNE 21<u>ST</u> 78.

Parole,   C. Sign, *Passaw.*

The Following Corps to be under Arms to Morrow
Morning and to March in the The Order which they
are Mentioned ye 20<u>th</u> of the Mounted Hessions
Waggons and all the Dismounted—The Queens Ran-
ger†—1 Officer and 20 With Waggons of the Ingi-
neers 1<u>st</u> Batln of Light Infantry. Queens Light
Dragoons—British Granneders Hessions Grannedeers
Two Medium 20 pounders. One Hautgers Brig<u>d</u> of
Guar<u>d</u> 3<u>d</u> Brigade of British 3<u>d</u> Batl<u>n</u> of the 4<u>th</u> Brigade
of British 6 pontoons The Remainder of the Ingineers
Intrinching Tools—Batt Horses of the Army Baggage
of the Gen<u>l</u> and Staff officer and the Army According
to the Line March—Cattle 5<u>th</u> Brigade of British
Hovenders‡ Troops Provential Cavelry are to be under
the Command of Brig<u>r</u> G<u>l</u> Lisley‖ The first Batl<u>n</u> of

———————

* "48th" in *Kemble Papers* (1, 596).

† The loyalist corps commanded by Lieut. Col. Simcoe.

‡ Capt. Richard Hovendon, commander of the troop of Provincial
Light Dragoon Cavalry.

‖ Alexander Leslie, commander of one of the three divisions of the
English Army.

the

the 4th Brigade is to flank the Baggage on the Left Lieut. Coll. Allens* will flank it on the Right and Lieut. Coll Vandikes Corps† will March in the Center of Baggage—The Remainder of the Army will Receive Order from his Excellency Lieut. Genl. Kniphosin.

John Fisher Drumant‡ in ye 28th Regt. . Tryed for Dissertion and Bearing Arms in the Rebels is found Guilty and Centanced to suffer Death he is to be Executed to Morrow on the March Between the Hours of 4 and 12.

HEAD QUARS. BLACK HORSE MONDAY JUNE 22D 1778.
    Parole, *Linion*.   Cs. *Essex*.

The Armey will March to morrow Morning in Two Coloms. Genl Lisleys Corps Reinforced by Hovenders Dragons Forming the Vance Guard of the Left Collom. Will be Ready to March at 2 OClock. The first Devision will form the Left Collom and Lay Ready to March.

---

* Lieut. Col. William Allen's corps of Pennsylvania Loyalists.

† Capt. J. Vandike, who by Howe's evidence had in May, 1778, "three troops of light dragoons, consisting of 132 troopers, and 174 real volunteers from Jersey." This corps was known as the "West Jersey Volunteers," and was either disbanded or merged in 1782, when Vandike was transferred to the Roman Catholic Volunteers.

‡ "John Fisher, Drummer," *Kemble Papers*, 1597.

HEAD QUAR^S CAMP AT CROSS WICKS JUNE 23^D 1778.

Parole, *Exeter*.   Cs. *Sunery*.

The Army will March to-morrow Morning—The Corps of Brig^{dr} Genl Lisleys Will if Possible joyn their Devission at Cross Wicks at 6 OClock. The Second Devission Under his Excellency Genl Kniphousen Will Begin his March at 4 OClock—the 1st Devission will Lie in Readiness to Move at 6 in the Same Order as this Day. The Houses of Swaill & Mr Tolmans* having Been Burnt This Morning. The

---

*Mrs. Shreve and Mr. Tallmans" in *Kemble Papers*. "The enemy on their way through Burlington County, wantonly destroyed a very valuable merchant mill near Bordentown, the iron works at Mountholly, and the dwelling-houses, out-houses, &c., of Peter Tallman, Esq., and Col. Shreve." *New Jersey Gazette*, June 24, 1778. Col. Caleb Shreve was at this time a representative in the Assembly, and Peter Tallman a representative in the Council of New Jersey. Though these are the only two buildings mentioned in the Orders, the following extract from *The New Jersey Gazette* of Aug. 5, shows much greater destruction during the retreat.

[Extract from a letter from Monmouth, dated July 18.]

"I have been waiting from the time the enemy passed thro' this country till the present, in expectation that some of your correspondents would, thro' the channel of your paper, have given the public an account of their conduct to the inhabitants—but not having seen any as yet, and as it has been such as every honest person ought to despise, I take this opportunity of giving a short sketch of it; which, if you think will be any satisfaction to your readers, you may insert in your paper. The devastation they have made in some parts of Freehold exceeds perhaps any they have made for the distance in their route thro' this State, having in the neighborhood above the Court-house burnt and destroyed eight dwelling houses, all on farms adjoining each other, besides

Commander

Commander In Chief Will if The Destruction of the Houses Was in Untonly* Given A Reward of 25 Guineys to Any Who Will Discover the Person Who sett Fire the Above Houses so that he may be Brought to A Punishment Diue to an Act so Disgracefull to the Army. The Commander In Chief Gives Notice that any Person Who may hereafter be found Committing such Disorders Will be Delivered to the Provost for Immediate Execution. Many of the Women who were Sent on Board the Transports

---

barns and out houses. The first they burnt was my own, then Benjamin Covenhoven's, George Walker's, Hannah Solomon's, Benjamin Van Cleav's, David Covenhoven's and Garrit Vanderveer's; John Benham's house and barn they wantonly tore and broke down so as to render them useless. It may not be improper to observe that the two first mentioned houses that were burnt adjoined the farm, and were in full view of the place where Gen. Clinton quartered. In the neighborhood below the Court-house they burnt the houses of Matthias Lane, Cornelius Covenhoven, John Antonidas, and one Emmans; these were burnt the morning before their defeat. Some have the effrontery to say, that the British officers by no means countenance or allow of burning. Did not the wanton burning of Charleston and Kingston in Esopus, besides many other instances, sufficiently evince the contrary, their conduct in Freehold I think may—the officers having been seen to exult at the sight of the flames, and heard to declare that they never could conquer America until they burnt every rebel's house, and murdered every man, woman and child. Besides, this consideration has great weight with me towards confirming the above, that after their defeat, thro' a retreat of twenty-five miles, in which they passed the houses of numbers well affected to their country, they never attempted to destroy one. Thus much for their burning."

* " Intentional " in *Kemble Papers.*

at

at Philadelphia being Present With the Armey. The Command^n Offir^s will Give in Returns as soon as may be Conveniant of The Number of Such Womin In their Respective Corps and They will specify by whome permission These Womin Regoined the Armey. The names Countys and Professions of all Followers of the Armey who are not all ready Regestred Must be Given into Capt Maddem of the 15th Reg^t Before to Morrow Evening—Army Genl. Kniphousens Orders Rechliston 23 June 1778. The Colum to March at 4 to Morrow morn^g In the same order as this day:—All the pioneers to march in the Rare of the 2^d Batl^n of Light Infentry Pioneers of the Reg^{ts} at the head of their Respective Brigades—The Rare Guards to Consist of the Reg^t Ducore* 49th & 4th British all The Batt [ery?] Horses of the Colums to March in the Frunt of the Generals Offr^s Baggage and on no Account to Mix With the Line of March.

MEMEM^R .

It is Required that any person That Lists A man that Want Two of His fingers on his Left Hand and has Mustered With the Armey from Philadel. Will secure him and Bring Him to Adj^t Genl.

---

*" Du corps," a Hessian regiment.

HEAD QUARS. EMELSTON [Emelstown] 24TH JUNE 1778.

Parole, *Nawfulk.*   C. S., *Munick.*

The Armey to March to Morrow Morning at 4 OClock In the same Order as this Day. The Rare Guard to Consist of The 55 & 58th Reg^t. Cliftons Corps* and The Jersey Vollinteers to flank the Right of the Artilreys Bagg^e, &c. The 5th, 10th, & Chalmers Corps to the Left.

HEAD QUARS. FREEHOLD TOWN SHIP 25TH JUNE 1778.

Parole, *Oxford.*   C. S., *Manhaim.*

The Colum to March to Mor^w Morning at 4 OClock in the Same Order as this Day—the Rare Guard to Consist of the 1st Bat^n Loues$\dagger$ Brig^{de} 27th British. Mounted yaugers 10th 23^d & Chalmers Corps on the Left flank of the Artilrey &c. Cliftons & Jersey Vollinteers up^n the Right. Half of the 17th Light Dragoons in the Rare of the Hessions. 1st troop in Rare of the Artilrey to Give their Attention to their left flank, the Remainder of the 17th Dragoons in Rare of the Light Infantry. A Detatchment of a 150 Men from Chalmers Corps to be in frunt of 4th Reg^t. under The Command of Coll. Innis.$\ddagger$

---

* Provincial corps of " Roman Catholic Volunteers," commanded by Lieut. Colonel Alfred Clifton, numbering, according to Howe's testimony, 180 men.

† Probably the Hessian battalion commanded by Col. John A. de Loos.

‡ Colonel Alexander Innes.

Head Quar.^s Camp Near frehold 26th June 1778.

Parole, *Leicester*. C. S., *Bonn*.

The Armey Will Remain to Morrow in its Present possition. One Days fresh and one Days Salt Provision Will be Isued to the Troops early to mor^w Morning.

The Genl Court Marshal which Lieu^t. Coll. [James] Grant is President is Disolved a Genl Court Marshal Consisting of 3 Field Offic.^r and 10 Captns. from the British to assemble at 8 OClock to Morrow Morning Near Head Quar^s. for the trial of such prisoners as May be Brought Before them.

Lieu^t. Coll. [Normand] Lamont President.

Lieu^t. Coll Dunkan.

L^t. coll. [Henry] Hope.

	Capts.
British Gran^{ds}	2
1st Batlⁿ	2
2 Brig^{de}	1
3d Brig^{de}	2
4 Brig^{de}	2
5 Brig^{de}	1

Total 3F. Offi^{rs} . . . . 10 Capt.

Capt. Addie* Judge advocate to whome the Dates of Commissioners are to be sent Early to Morning. Field officer British Lines Lt. Coll. Trelaney.† MB.

---

*Capt. Stephen Payne Adye.

† Henry Trelawney?

Stephens

Stephens.   Memm. the Pickets of the whole Armey to
Mount to Morrow Morning at Gun fire.

Coll. Chalmers will please to Order such Evidences
to Prossicute the Prisioners Charg^d with Burning
Houses this Day.

Lost on the March yesterday A silver pistole who
ever will Bring it to the adj^t of 2^d Infantry will Receive One Guiney Reward.   Two Horses to be Sold at
Coll. Lowstint.

ORDERS.

The Next Detatchment Ordered from Lieu^t Coll.
Chalmers Corps for Safe Guards will be devided into
Non Commission^d Officers Guards of a sergt. or
Corp^l. and 4 privates.   They will fall in Regulerly to
be Ready to fall out when Cald on—and be distin-
guished by G^d N° 1, 2, 3, &c.   A Subalton Officer to
Remain with every 4 of these Guards, and A Capt
With Every 8, if any of the Houses they protect are
fixed on for Quar^s for Genl. Offi^{rs} they are to admitt
of a Centry being poasted with them but are not to
Move till Ordered By the Genl. Offi^r or his Aide
Camp or Brigade Major.   In houses upon the Road
out of the Line of Qua^{rs} the Safe G^d is to Remain till
the Rare gua^d of the Armey passes thin to join them
and proceed to their Detatchment.   A Report to the
Commanding Offic^r if any Disorderly people attempt-
ing to force the safe Guards into Plunder Where they
are poasted The guards is Imediately Make them
Prisoners

Prisoners and fire on them if they should Make Resistance, if any Reinforcement of the safe Guards should be Wanting Application to be made to the Command^n Officer of the next Batt^n —The Inhabitants Must be Desired to Drive their Cattel into a proper Inclosier that such as are fitted for the use ot the armey May be Delivere^d to the assistants to the Commissa^ry Genl who will pay a Reasonable price for them—all Womin following the armey and Other Stragglers who attempt Coming on the rare of ye army Houses Barns or Other Buildins will be secured for Leaveing the Line of March wheather they Commit any Disorders or not.

R[egimental] O[rder] Every Officer in the Battn to have a Coppy of this order.

R. O. No Officer or Solder to Quitt his poast Devision Platoon or Command on any account Whatever.

HEAD QUAR^S CAMP FREHOLD JUNE 27TH 1778.

Parole, *Berwick.* C Sign, *Coblentz.*

The Armey to Move to Morrow Morning at 3 OClock—

Genl. Kniphousins Orders.

CAMP MIDDLETON JUNE 28ᵀᴴ 1778.*

Parole, *Clinton.*   C Sign, *New York.*

Coll⁰ Chalmers Corps Cliftons & Vandikes to Remain on their preasant Ground till further orders.

HEAD QUARˢ MIDDLETON JUNE 29th 1778.

Parole, *Bedford.*   C S *Lissa—*

CAMP NEAR MIDDLETON JUNE 30ᵀᴴ 1778.

Parole, *Darby.*   C. Sign, *Pina.*

MORNING ORDERS JULY YE Iˢᵀ 1778.

Officers Commanding Corps Will as soon as possible Will give into Majr Brewen† D[eputy] Qʳ Master Genˡ, A Return for Embarkation of all Horses in their Respective Corps Consistint with the Regularety. No provision Can be Made for the Transportation of any Other horses.

Parole, *Leeds*   C Sign *Fulda.*

HEADQUARˢ CAMP [NEAR NEVERSINK] JULY 2ᴰ 1778.

Parole,   C. S. *Molwitz.*

The baggage of the armey to be embarked to Morrow morning as Early as possable—Two days salt

---

* On this day the battle of Monmouth was fought, the chief brunt being borne by Knyphausen's division.

† Henry Bruen.

Provisions

Provisions Bread and Rum to be Served to the troops
to morrow Morning to the 4th Instant at the Place of
Embarkation—A Return Horses for Embarkn Be-
longn to the Genl and staff Offirs of the Armey to be
Given in this Night to Majr Brewen Dey Qr Mr Genl

For the British Lines this Evening Coll Stephns.

Packet Will Sale for Europe in a few Days.

HEAD QUARS CAMP JULY 3D 1778.

Parole, C Sign, *Olmutz.*

One Days fresh provision will be Ishued to the
Officers of the armey to Morrow Morning.

Chaddock Buttler* Tryed by the Genl Cort Marshal
of which Lt Coll Lamont was president for stealing a
Horse is found not guilty and therefore Acquited.

Michal Peperly and addam Derry Driver in the Qr
Masr Genl Depart Tryed for seting to and Burning
Houses are found not Guilty and Therefore Acquited.

Mary Coulfritt† and Elizabeth Clark followers of
the armey Tryed for Plundering.

The Court is of the Oppinion That Mary Colfritt is
not Guilty—But that Elizabeth Clark is Guilty and Do
therefore Adjudge her to Receive 100 Lashes on her
Bear Back and to be Drumd out of the armey in the
Most Publick manner—The Commandr in Chief Con-
ferms the above Centence.

*" Chadlock Butler," in *Kemble Papers.*
†" Mary Colethrate," in *Kemble Papers.*

All

All Horses and Waggons Belonging to Q<u>r</u>. Mas<u>r</u>. Gen<u>l</u>. Department in posseation of Difrant Officers of Corps or Departments of the Armey are to be delivered up to Morrow Morning at 5 OClock at the New Bridge Leading to The Hook Where an Officer at That Department Will Receive them—For the B. Lines this Evening Coll<u>o</u> O'Harow.* The Pa<u>t</u>. Officer of the Line found a B<u>r</u>. Rone with a saddle and Cloak The Owner Will Apply to Lt. Coll. Worns.*

R.O. For Duty this Evening Capt. G[rafton] Dulaney & Lt. Sinclier [James Sinclair].

HEAD QUAR<u>S</u>. CAMP NEAR SANDY HOOK
JULY 4TH, 1778.

Parole, C. Sign, *Mints*.

The Armey will hold itself in Readiness to March at Daybrake to Morrow—all followers of The armey who wish to Embark With it from hence are to apply for Passes to Capt Madden Superintended of Refugees —For the British Lines this Eveng. Coll. [Richard] Prestcot.

SANDY HOOK JULY 5TH, 1778.

Parole, *Suffolk*. C S., *frankfort*.

The March Being Now Complated The Commander In Chief Desires to Return his thanks to the army for

---

* James O'Hara.
† Lieut. Col. Philip von Wurmb.

the

the Cherefulness which they Have Supported The
fatiges of the Duty. He wishes Likewise to Deliver
his satisfaction at the Noble Orders Shown by that part
of the Armey who Repulsed suppersition Numbers of
the Enemy the 28th of June. And on this Occation
The Commander in Chief Most begs Leave to Express
his Sence of the Assistance Receiv^d from the Zeal of
Lt Genl Lord Cornwallis & Maj^r Genl Gray Brigd^r
Genl Mathews & Sir Wm. Erskins. The Commander
in Chief is then with Realtery [reluctance ?] Oblidg^d
to say that the Irregularity of the Armey During the
March Reflected Much Disgrace On that Discipling
what aught to be the first Object of an Offi^{rs}

Attention—The flank Companys of all the British
Reg^{ts} of this Devision of the Armey are to join their
Respective Corps till further Orders.

The flanking Companys of the 22 & 23 Reg^t will
Remain Embodied under the Command of the Oldest
Officer.

The 1st & 2^d Brig^{des} of British are to Encamp Near
the water place On Staten Island butt They are not
to Land till they Receive their Tents.

The 16th & 17th Dragoons and 73* Dis^d Troops
the Guards flank Companies at [of?] the 22 & 43^d
Regts. A Murricans Queens Rangers and all the
Hession Corps to Be posted on N. York Island—the
Tents† of the Army will be Stationed Near Utrick On

---

* "And the three Provincial Troops" in *Kemble Papers*, 1, 603.

† " Rest" in *Kemble Papers*, 1, 603.

Long

Long Island—The Guns which have been Attach to particular Corps During the march are to Rejoin them as the Troops will Embark Immediately Their Provision will not be Isued to them till they Gitt on Board their Respective Transports.

R. O. For Duty this Evening Capt. Wal[te]r Dulaney L!̲ [Thomas H.] Parker.

Morning Orders july ye 6th 1778. The troops to Land as soon as Possable with two Days Provisn The Commanding Officers to be Anserable that no man Quits his Camp and that no Depredation are Committed on the Property of the Inhabitants—Either in Burneing or pulling Down fencing or taking furage of any kind as straw fuel and furage will be Regulerly Delivered.

The Regiments will not Land any Heavey Baggage Except Tents and Officers Nessisareys as Safe Guards are to be posted at Every House it is Expected that The Strictest attention will be paid to them as they have Orders to fire on any Person who attempts to force them.

Officers will Take Care that no Women are Landed on any Account Till the men are In Campt.

———

GENL. ORDERS GRAVESEND BAY JULY 7TH, 1778.

Parole, *Northumberland.*   C Sign, *Gray.*

The Inhabitants of that Land Gravesend & Without Yallow Hook are to furnish troops with wood and straw

straw According to the Regulation. But in the mean time The Commanding Officers of Reg^ts are to Give Receats for What they Receive—The 5th Brig^de to Apply to Maj^r Vanderbilt at flatt Lands. The 4th Brig^de to Mr. Cokerhove at whicht Land The Provencial Troops to Johanner Bergen at Yellow Hook. The Roads to be Calld frequently and Perticulerly in the afternoon it is Requested of Commanding Officers of Reg^t to keep their men from stragling out of the Camp in Case of no Commissary not attending the Defferent Brig^ds The Commanding Officers of Reg^ts will give Recepts for any furage that may be Received from any of the Inhabitants Attending that the Quarters Dose not Exceed the Embarkation Return of Horses Given in to the Q^r Mr Genl [Sir William Erskine] to Morrow—Waggons will Attend to morrow to Bring up Baggage of the Armey according to their Allowance. Spaceing this Days Orders. The Women of the armey are permit^d to join their Reg^ts to morrow—Sir William Arskins Brigideer Genl.

HEAD QUAR^s JULY 8TH, 1778.
Parole, *Obdeek.*   C Sign *Uxburge.*
The troops Incampt at or near Kings Bridge are upon no Account to Cutt Down or Distroy the Hemp or Spruce Growing in the Woods in the Neighberhood Except by an Order from Mr. Lutwige* Superintended

---

* Edward Goldstone Lutwyche, of New Hampshire, (*Parliamentary*

of

of the Kings Braverry Commanding Officers of Corps are Requested to be Perticularly Attentive to These Orders as the Preservation of the Spruce is of Utmost Consiquence to the Troops.

All Convelants and Recrutes 'at New York Paul[u]s Hook or Stratton Island are to be Immediately sent for by their Respective Reg^ts .

The Convelaisants of New York are under The Directions of the Town Adj^t .

Such Corps or Departments have not allready settled their stoppages with the Pervaior of his Majestys Hospittal to Comply with this Order Immediately.

The Reg^t of Merbeck* to March to Morrow morning as Early as Possible to New York and In Camp on the Ground Lately Occupied By the 33^d Reg^t .

HEAD QUAR^S JULY 9TH 1778.†

Morning Orders July 12th, 1778.

Regimental Coart Marshall to set Immediately.

Register, xi. 198), who in 1778 was "superintendant of the Kings Brewery at New York," being paid at the rate of 10 / per day. The timber was wanted to brew spruce beer, for the purpose of preventing scurvy, very prevalent in the army from the necessity of feeding the troops with salt meats.

* Mirbeck.

† Here follow six blank pages in the original MS.

Capt.

Capt. Key* President.

Lt. Townsin. } Members. { Lt. Ingils.
Ens. Jones. { Ens. McPherson.

HEAD QUARS. NEW YORK JULY 12TH, 1778.
Parole,   C Sign.

HEAD QUARS. NEW YORK JULY 13,
Parole, *Sotza.*   C Sign, *Atton.*

14TH JULY 1778.

A Regimental Coart Martial to set this morning
Immediately.

Capt. Key President.

Lt. Starling. } Members. { Lt. Parker.
Ens. Monrow. { Ens. Bowls. †

The Battn. to Perade at troop Beating Every Morning for Exercize Offirs. Servants to attend the Battn.
Men and Pioneers to attend the Drill in the Evenings
the Orderly Corpl. to Parade their men and the aukerd
men of their Respective Companys and assist the
Drill Sergt. in Teaching them no man to appear on A
Perade or beyond the Sentreys of the Battn. without
being uniformly Dressed. When the men Perade

---

* Philip Barton Key, afterwards member of Congress. See *Sabine.*

† William Augustus Bowles, who afterwards became notorious as
" Commander in Chief of the Creek Nation." See *Authentic Memoirs
of* . . . London 1791; *Public Characters* for 1801-2; and *Sabine.*

under

under Arms the Offic^{rs} to have their fire arms. When the Battⁿ exersize an Officer of a Company to be anserablee that the men present are in Good Order and the absent men Duley Reported as the Compan^s Must Account for all their Arms by them Received they are forthwith to put thier Spear [spare] arms in the Best Order as the Whole are to be Inspected next friday. The mens accounts to made up to the 24 of June in Order to have them Cleared With how Soon the nessasar^s Wanting are Provided.

No man of What Ever Rank to Leave the Camp without proper Leave. No Man to take his fire Lock to Peices Except taking of the Lock on Any Acc^t What Ever Without Leave from an Off^r who is to be Answerable that the Brich is not taken out nor the Stock Distroyed—

The Q^r M^r to be answerable the Incampment is swept Clean every morning that is from Tents of Staff to ten yards Behind the Quart^r Guard.

HEAD QUART^{RS} DURRYEES HOUSE LONG ISLAND
JULY 14TH 1778.
Parole, *Bagshot.*   C S, *Sticklinburg.*

HEAD QUART^{RS} DURYEES HOUSE JULY 15TH, 1778.
Parole, *Portsmouth.*   C Sign, *Stettin.*
R. O. Officer for Guard is to March of the Guard and Contineu with it During the 24 Hours.

For

For Guard this Day Lieut. Townsin for to Morrow
Enˢ Jones.

HEAD QUARTᴿˢ JULY 16ᵀᴴ, 1778.

Parole, *Dorset.*   C Sign, *Frelenhousan.*

R. O.   For Guard to Morrow Lᵗ Ingils.

Morning Orders July 17th A Regimental Coart
matial to set Immediately.

Capt. Coston President.

Enˢ Jones, ⎫   ⎧ Lᵗ Townsin,
Lᵗ Starlin, ⎭ Members. ⎨ Lᵗ Sinclier.

HEAD QUARˢ NEW YORK JULY 17ᵀᴴ 78.

Parole,   C Sign.

R. O for Guard to Morrow Enˢ Starling.

HEAD QUARS. NEW YORK JULY 18ᵀᴴ 1778.

Parole, *Northampton.*   C Sign, *Mores.*

R. O. for gard to Morrow Lᵗ Sinclier.

HEAD QUARˢ NEW YORK JULY 19ᵀᴴ 1778.

Parole, *Exeter.*   C Sign, *Arras.*

When Small Detatchments are Sent from Any Corps
the Commanding Officers of That Corps is to send
With them A Certificate Spacifying to what Time they
                                                          are

are Victualed as the Commassarys are Desired not to
Give any Provision to them Till further Orders. The
Troops to Receive 2 Days Rice instead of flower.
The corps of Pioneers and Others so Acting in futer
to Receive the Same Proportion of Rum that the Soldiers do—The Packet will sale for Europe this Ensu-
ing Weak the Exact time of her Departure is Unex-
pected all Letters Intended to be Sent are to be Sent
to the Town Mag^r in fair street on or before sundy
Next at which time the male will be Cleared—The
Commissary [Daniel Weir] Will begin Mustering the
Reg^{ts} Stationed on Strattin Island on Mon Day the
20th july, and these on Long Island the Saterday following the Weather Permitting.

R. O. For Guard to Morrow En^s Mc Pherson.

HEAD QUAR^s NEW YORK JULY 20TH 1778.

Parole, *Cornwallis*. C Sign, *Friburg*.

Such field Offciers Commanding Offi^{rs} of Corps &
Staff officers who have had their Herses keld in
Action are to Apply for paym^t for the Rate of £15
Each—at the Quarter Master Genl Office. A Num-
ber of Officers Tents and Marquees being Sent from
Ingland For the Use of the Armey Such Corps as
are in Want of them will Apply to the Q^r Mr Genl
Office—The payment of Such Corps as Receive them
will transmitt to their Respective Agents the Names
of the Officers they are Delivered to in Order that the

Proper

Proper stoppages may be made—Mr. John Craige* is Oppointed to Act in the Q^r Mr Generals Office. The Commander in Chief being Informed it Was his Excellency Sr Wm Howes Intention that Lieu^t Coll Simcoe† of the Queens Rangers Should have Rank of all Lieu^t Collonlls of Provincials in this Establishment and Being Convinced of the Justice of the Measure—it is His Excellenceys Pleasure That Lieu^t Colonell Simcoe should take Rank in Provencial Servise from the 1st July 1776—The Troops to Receive two Days provision to the 22^d july tomorrow Morning flower to be Ishued instead of Bread.

R. O. For Gd. to mw. Lt Parker.

NEW YORK JULY 21ST 1778.

The Penns^y Loyalists and M^d Loyalists & R C Vollinteers‡ are to hold them Selves in Readiness to March they will Receive further Orders from Major Genl Tryon‖ Under whose Command they are to put themselves.§ Sign^d Rawdon adj^t Genl

---

* *Sabine* mentions a John Craig who went with his family and three servants to Shelburne, N. S., in 1783.

† John Graves Simcoe.

‡ "Roman Catholic Volunteers." See *Gaine's Gazette*, July 13, 1778.

‖ Major General in the British forces, in command of the loyalist forces.

§ This included Allen's, Chalmers', and Clifton's corps, numbering about 700 men.

R. O.

R. O. when the Battⁿ march all Officers servants and Battⁿ men to Carry their arms and fall into the Ranks—The pioneers to attend the Q^r M^r with their arms. A Return of spear arms in Each Company.
For Guard to Morrow En^s Bowls.

NEW YORK JULY 22 1778.

Major Genl Tryons Orders Lt Coll^o Chalmers Battⁿ to march Early to morrow morning and Encamp Near Jamacea and on friday will Proceed by force Marches to huntington Where they Will Encamp and Waitt there for further Orders. The strictest Disapline will be Maintained—it is Recommended to the Officers to take as Little Baggage as Possable the service they are going upon making it Nessary.

Fore Days provisions to be taken With the Reg^t. Lt Chalmers will apply to Coll. Axtill* for press Waggons to Carry the same as also the Sick that Can be Moved which may be Left at the Village of Hirricks Bay† and Jameacca with a proper Non Commissioned Officer, till able to join the Reg^t. Lt Coll. Chalmers will apply to the Q^r Mr Genl for Such waggns as are Allowed by Genl Orders to Carry the Baggage.

R. O. The Heavy Baggage of the Battⁿ to be Col-

---

*Col. William Axtell. See *Sabine*, I, 198; Thompson's *Long Island*, I, 226, 228, and Onderdonk's *Revolutionary Incidents of Suffolk and Kings Counties*, 167, 172, 175, 184, 187.

† In North Hempstead township.

lected

lected in the Center of the Reg^t by the Q^r M^r and Left in Ceare of the Q^r G^d   The tents to be struck at ½ after 3 tomorrow morning and to be Ready to March of at 4.

HEAD QUAR^S NEW YORK JULY 23^D 1778.
Parole, *Cambridge.*   C S *Narcea.*
R. O. for Guard to morrow En^s Jones.
A Reg^{tl} Court Martial to sett to morrow morning at 9 O'Clock.

Capt. G. Dulany President.

En^s McPherson, ⎫ Members, ⎰ Lt Ingils,
En^s Starling,   ⎭   ⎱ Lt. Parker,

HEAD QUAR^S NEW YORK JULY 25TH, 1778.
Parole, *Falmouth.*   C. Sign, *Lutzer.*
R. O. for Guard to Morrow En^s Jones.

HEAD QUAR^S NEW YORK JULY 26TH 1778.
Parole,   C S.
The Muster Mas^r Genl of Provential will begin to Muster the provencial Corps In New York Islant to morrow the 27th Instant—The Q^r Mas^r of the different Corps that Came from Philadelphia are to Attend at the Barrick Office in Mayden Ally New York Any Day

Day betwen this and first of Augt to settle their Barrick and fuel act^s with Capt Pain.*

R. O. for g^d to morrow Ens. McPherson.

HEAD QUAR^s NEW YORK JULY 27TH 1778.

Parole,   C Sign, *Lissa.*

No Soldiers is hereafter to Leave the Camp at Brooklin without a pass sign^d by an Officer and the Soldiers not to pay for their passage nor Officer when going on Duty. The boats are not to pass or Repass after 9 at Night butt In Case of an Express.

R. O. for Gu^d to morrow En^s Starling.†

R. O. 29th 1778. The Tents to be Struck to morrow morning at 3 O'Clock and the Battn. to March of at 4. fore Day provision to be Carried with the Regt. 1 Subolt on and 16 men to Remain On the Ground till the whole Baggage is March. No man to Appear on the march without Arms as no Excuse of Being Absent. Battn. men Baggage men or pioneers will be Allowed.

CAMP JERICHO LONG ISLAND JULY 30TH 1778.

Parole,   C Sign.

The Reg^t to march to Morrow at 4 OClock.

* James Paine?

† Two and a half blank pages follow in the MS.

CAMP JERICHO LONG ISLAND JULY 30ᵀᴴ.

Parole,   C Sign.

The tents to be struck to morrow morning at Revallee Beating and the Regᵗ to march of at 4 O'Clock Every man able to Carry arms to fall in to the Ranks and Contineu with the Battⁿ During the Days march The sergen to attend the sick and to be anseable that the Mateneos[?] are not allowed in the Number of sick Reports to the Commanding Officers. It is again Ordered the Officers march with their Companeys and be Anserable that No man Quitt his Ranks Except in Case of Sickness.

HEAD QUARˢ HUNTINGTON JULY 31ˢᵀ 1778.

Parole,   C Sign.

Field Officer for Duty this Day Lᵗ Coll [Richard] Hewlett,* for to mʷ Major Minzies.†

Comp Gᵈ and sentres as usuˡ for the securety of Each Corps to furnish a Capᵗ of the Day as in the former Encampment who are to Superintend and Report the Inline Picket Besides which an outline picket

---

* Of Hempstead, N. Y., Colonel of De Lancey's 3rd battalion. See *Sabine* II, 532. In 1776 he was reported to the Committee of Newtown as "an active and bitter enemy of his Country." Cf. Thompson's *Long Island*, I, 200, 205; Onderdonk's *Revolutionary Incidents of Suffolk and Kings Counties*, 65, 70; Onderdonk's *Revolutionary Incidents of Queens County*, 42, 192.

† Major Alexander Menzies, of De Lancey's 3d battalion.

Consisting

Consisting of 1^s 1^s 2^l & 20 pr^{ts} will mount at Sun Sett at the Cross Roads Between Platts town and Wickes Common. 1st Batt^n Dulanceys giveing the Outline Picket this Evening, at the same time the 3^d Batt^n will furnish a guard of a Corp^l and 6 privates at Brig^{dr} Genl Dulanceys* Quar^s which will be Releaved by the 1st Batt^n to m^w morning. No Inhabitants to Receive more than 4 Coppers pr Quart for milk—The fencis are not to be Distroyed nor Burntt and the Q^r, Master are Desired to Apply to Justice Platt for fuell for the Necessaryes of the Camp. No tavern keper or Inhabitants to persume to sell Rum or any Other spiritual Licquers but By a written ordr produced from an Officer.

After Orders A Corpl. & 6 to mount Immediately at Major Genl Tryon Quar^s from 1st Batt^n Dullanceys and to be Releaved by an Eaqual N^o from the 3 Batt^n tom^w Morning.

HEAD QUAR^s AUG^T 1ST 1778.

Parole, *Cavilt.*　　　　　C Sign, *Boyn.*

Field Officer for Duty tom^w Lt Coll. Cruger.†
Adj^t for the Day 1st B Dulanceys for to Morrow from

---

* Oliver De Lancey, Commander of the three batallions of New York loyalists known as De Lancey's Brigade, numbering in May, 1778, according to Howe's testimony some 707.

† John Harris Cruger, commander of DeLancey's 1st Battalion. See *Sabine,* I, 344.

the

the 3ᵈ Do. Outline Pickett this Evening On the Right
of the Encampment

S	S	C		R & file	
1	1	1	&	16 . . .	from 3ᵈ Battn.
0	0	1	&	4 . . .	from 1ˢᵗ Do.
1	1	2	&	20	

Genˡ Tryons Guard of a Corpˡ and 6 to morrow from
1ˢᵗ B Dullanceys. Brigᵈʳ Genl. Dulancey D Gᵈ from
the 3ᵈ Battⁿ .

Brigade Major Waller* to Act as Adjᵗ Genˡ to the
Command under Genˡ Tryon. The two field peices
Escorted by Coll. Chalmers Battⁿ to be sent to the
1ˢᵗ Battⁿ Dulanceys as soon as they are arrived in
Camp.

A Return to be Given in Immediately from Each
Corps of the Names and Numbers of the men who
have been on Command with the artillery. Returns
to be Given in at the Same time of the No of men
who have not Recieved Cloathing in Coll. Chalmers
& Cliftons Battⁿ as also what arm are wanting or Sup-
pernumery to Each.—The Maryland Loyalists and
R. C. Vollinteers to march to Morrow Morning at 5
O'Clock to Smyths Town where they will in Camp.

The troops will Constantly March (where the Ground
will admitt of it) by half Companys. The Genˡ Ex-

*John Waller, Brigade Major under Tryon. *Sabine* erroneously
states that he was a Major in Delancey's Brigade.

pects

pects the Officers will March with thier Devissions and not suffer their men to straggle from them under any Pertance.

An Out Line Picket to be maned[?] on the Heights on the Left of the Encampments of the Batt^n that Arrived to Day Consisting of 1^s 1^s 2^c & 20 p^t from M^d Loyalists at sun set this Evening which will Joyn its Corps at Day Brake.

In the Morning.

The Assistant Qua^r Master Genl to furnish 5 Waggons to the 1st Batt^n Dulanceys and Coll^o Corps Each, and to the 3^d B and Coll. Cliftons 4 Each—Orderly Serg^t tom^w to Genl Tryon from 1st B Dulanceys D^o to Major Brig^de 3^d B. D^o .

R. O. for Pickett this Evening Lt Starling for the Inline Pickett Lt Ingils—Capt for the Day Capt G^d Dulaney.

Head Quar^s . Hunting—After Orders 3 OClock. 1 Subalton 1 Sergt. and 20 Rank an file from M Loyalists to march to Ridoupts at Loyds Neck to morrow morning in Order to Embark on Board the Union Armed transport as soon as she arrives and Releave a Detachment of Loyal A Merricans Regt.* Now on Board which is to join its Reg^t at Flushin fly.

---

* The regiment commanded by Beverly Robinson.

CAMP SMYTHS TOWN AUG.ᵗ 2.ᴰ 78.

R. O. A Reg.ᵗ Coart Martial to set to Morrow morning at 6 OClock.

Capt. W. Dulaney, President.

Enˢ. Bowls ⎱ Members. ⎰ Enˢ. Monrow,
Lt. Sinclier ⎰ ⎱ Lᵗ. Starling.

for guard this Evening Lᵗ. Townsin for the Inline Pickett Enˢ. Mᶜ Pherson.

HEAD QUARˢ. SMYTHS TOWN, AUG.ᵗ 3.ᴰ 1778.

Parole, C S

Field Officer for Duty to Morrow Lt. Chalmers adjᵗ. 3.ᵈ Battⁿ. Dullanceys.

The field Officer on Duty to Direct the poasting of the Outline picketts and of the Orders Respecting Rounds and Patroles.

The Inline Picketts of 1.ˢᵗ Battⁿ and Mariland Loyalists to consist of 1ˢ. 1ˢ. 1ᵈ & 25 Rank & file Each, and those of the 3d Battn. Dulanceys R. C. Vollinteers 1ˢ. 1ˢ. 1ᵈ & 20 Rank and file under the Inspection of a Capt. of the Day wich Each Corps will Constant and who is to Report Every Morning to the field Officer on Duty

C.	S.	S.	D.	R & F.
1	2	2	1.	50

from the two Battn. of Dulanceys Brigade to Morrow,

an

an outline Pickett this Evening in the Rare of the
Camp. Detale

	C.	S.	S.	D.	R & F.
1st B Dulanceys. . .	1	0	1	1	30.
3d Battn. Do.	0	2	1		20.
Total	1	2	2	1	50.

The Mariland Loyalists and R. C. V. to mount on
outline pickett Consisting of the above Number
Detale.

	C.	S.	S.	D.	R.
Mal^d Loyalists . . .	0	1	1	1.	30.
R. C. Vollonteers . .	1	1	1	0.	20.
Total	1	2	2	1.	50.

Sr. Henrey Clinton has been Pleased to Order that
the three Militia Light Troops should furnish their
Own Provision while on this Service and while Embodied both. Officer and men are to Receive full Pay
as Light Draggons and have a wagon allowed to each
Troop to Carry their Provision Genl Tryon Orders
the 3 Troops to be formed in one Squadron undr the
Command of Coll. Hamelton* who will make all Returns Cal^d for to Major Waller adj^t Genl The Troops
to march to moro^w morning at 2 O Clock in the following Orders R. C. V. and Capt. Kenlocks† Troop

---

* Probably Archibald Hamilton.

† A troop raised on Long Island early in 1778. Cf. Onderdonk's
Revolutionary Incidents in Queens County, 156.

to

to furnish the Vanc Guard— The Inf$\underset{.}{y}$ to lead—The two Battn Dulanceys and Mariland Loyalists to main body—Coll. Hameltons furnysh the Van Guard.

The Common Commissary and Waggons as Ordered yesterday A Sub$\underset{.}{n}$ and 20 men of R. C. V. to Advance in frunt of the Vanc Guard—on the march each Corps to furnish its own flanker.

R.O. For Duty this Evening for the Inline pickett Capt Key and Lt. Sinclier—for the Outline Pickett Lt. Ingils.

HEAD QUAR$^\underline{s}$ SATUCKETT AUG$^\underset{.}{t}$ 4TH 1778.

Field Officer for Duty to morrow Major [John] Lynch adj$^{t}_{.}$ M. Loyalists Gen$^{l}_{.}$ Tryons G^{d} this Day 1st B. Dulanceys to morrow M—Loyalists Brig^{dr} Gen$^{l}_{.}$ Dulanceys G^{d} of a Corpral and 6 privates from the 3^{d} Batt$^{n}_{.}$ Dulanceys to Morrow R: C. Vollonteers—Detale for outline pickett this Evening.

	C.	S.	S.	D.	R & F.
1$^{st}_{.}$ B Dulanceys . .	1	1	2	1.	30.
3^{d} Batt^{n} Do	1	0	0	0.	20.
M. Loyalists	0	2	2	1.	30.
R. C. Vollinteers . .	0	1	0	0.	20.
Total	2	4	4	2.	100.

Orderly Serg^{t} at Head Quars this Day 1st Batt^{n} Dulanceys to morrow M^{d} Loyalists—Two Days fresh Provision

Provision is to be Delivered to the Troops to Morrow
—A Pickett from Coll. Hameltons squadron to Consist
of $1-S -1-S -1-D$ & 19 Rank & file to Mount Every
Evening at Sun Sett at Crains Neck and to the Report
to the field Officer of the Day. The squaddrens will
also furnish patroles for the Camp The Quarter Guard
to furnish each a Sentry towards the water side from
hence all Boats are to Be Drawn up so they are not
Liable to be Landed without the nowligee of the sentry.

R. O. for the Outline pickett this Evening En[s]
Mcpherson and L[t] Sinclier for the Inline pickett Cap[t]
Coston and En[s] Bowls.

———

HEAD QUAR[s] SATUCKETT AUG[T] 5TH 1778.

Parole, *Clinton*.   C Sign.

Field Officer for Duty to Morrow Lt. Coll Clifton
Adg[t] from R. C. Vollinteers Gen[l] Tryons G[d] from
the 1st Batt[n] Dulanceys Brig[dr] Gen[l] Dullanceys G[d]
3[d] Batt[n] D[o] Orderly serg[t] head q[r] from 3[d] Batt[n] D[o].
· Detail for the Outpickett this Evening.

	C.	S.	S.	D.	R & file.
1st Batt[n] Dulancey .	0	1	1	0.	30.
3[d] Batt[n] D[o]	0	1	1	0.	20.
M. Loyalists . . .	1	1	1	1.	30.
R. C. Vol[ns]	1	1	1	1.	20.
Total	2	4	4	2.	100.

The

The Genl. Expects that every Officer will keep in Camp and that no One puts his name on a house for the Purpose of taking it for Quarters.—The Qua^r. M^r. Genl. only is allowed to do that for such as are intitleed to Quarters and who are to Make applytion to him in Order to Obtain them.

Prices of Provisions in suffick County to be Observed By the Troops till further Orders.

Weathers . . . . at . . . 32 shillings.
Ewes . . . . at . . . 25 D^o
Lambs . . . . at . . . 20 D^o
Turkeys . . . . . . at . . . 5
Fowles . . . . at . . . 3 Do.
Geese . . . . at . . . 4 Do.
Ducks . . . . at . . . 2 / 3 D^o
fowles . . . . at . . . 1 / 9 D^o
Chickins . . . . . . at . . . 1 / 8 D^o
Beaf . . . . at . . . .10 pr. Pound.
Veal . . . . at . . . 1 shilling.
Pork . . . . at . . . 1 D^o
fresh butter . . . . . at . . . 1 / 6 D^o
Eggs . . . . 8 for 1 / 3 D^o
Milk pr. Quart . . . . 3 Coppers.
Wheat pr. Bush^l . . . . . . 12 shillings.
Rey . . . . at . . . 7 shillings.
Indian Corn . . . . . at . . . 7 D^o
Old Oats . . . . . . at . . . 5 D^o
New Do . . . . . . at . . . 4 / 6 D^o

Flower

Flower . . . . at . . . 35 Do.
Cyder Pr Bal . . . . . at . . . 30 D?
D? Pr Qr . . . . at . . . 6

R O. For the Outline Pickitt This Evening Cap.ᵗ
frisby and En.ˢ Bowls. for the Inline Cap.ᵗ Walter Dulaney and L.ᵗ parker.

HEAD QUAR.ˢ SATUCKETT AUG.ᵀ 6ᵀᴴ 1778.
Parole, *Hess.*   C. Sign,

Field Officer For Duty to Morrow Major Mc Daniald* adj.ᵗ M.ᵈ Loyalists.

Detail for Out Pickett this Evening.

·	C.	S.	S.	D.	R & F.
M. Loyalists	o	2	1	1.	30.
R. C. Vollon.ᵗ . . .	o	o	1	o.	20.
Total	o	2	2	1.	50.

The Troops to be in Readiness to March in An
hours Notice.

R. O. For the Out pickett L.ᵗ Parker and En.ˢ.ᵎ
Morrow. For the Inline pickett Capt. W. Dulaney
and L.ᵗ Starling.

Corpl. Thom.ˢ Gill of Cap.ᵗ W. Dulaneys Company
is Oppoynted Serg.ᵗ in Cap.ᵗ frisbys Comp.ʸ.

---

* John McDonald, of the "Maryland Loyalists."

HEAD QUAR^S WEIDEN RIVER AUG^T 7TH, 1778.

Parole, *Weiden.*   C. Sign, *Hudson.*

Field Officer for Duty to morrow Lt Coll. Hulett Adj^t 1st Battⁿ Dulanceys The Out pickett Ordered this Evening as Last Night—A G^d of a Serg^t and Corpral & 12 to Mount at Head Quar^s Emmediately.

	C.	S.	S.	D.	R.
Mar^d Loyalists . . .	0	1	0	0.	8.
R. C. V.	0	0	1	0.	4.
	0	1	1	0.	12.

A Pickitt of an Officer & 30 from Coll^o Hameltons Squaddrun to Mount this Evening On the hill In the Rare of the Camp Sentries During the Night. The Genl is so Sorrey to have Occation to Take Notise of the Sorrey Scanderlus and Irregular Behavier of Some Disorderly Soldiers. The full Confidance he has in the Spiritt of all the corps under his Command will Intitle him to the Zealus Exertion of the Officers and a punctual Obedience from the Soldiers in the Reguard of thier Duty.

No Soldier to be allowed to go In a House—The troops to March to morrow morning at 4 O'Clock— The Order of the march is as Strict as yesterday.

R. O. For the Outline pickett this Night Lt Parker and En^s Monrow—for the Inline Duty Capt Jones and Lt Starling.

HEAD QUARS. MATITUCK, AUGT 8, 78.

Field Officer for the Day Lt Coll Cruger Adjt 1st Battn Dulanceys. Field Officer for to Morrow Major Lynch. Adjt 3 B. Dulany Gd. at Head Quars this Day one Sergt 1 Corpl & 12 from 1st Battn Dulanceys. Do at Head Quars to Morrow M Loyalist Brigdr. Genl. Dulanceys Gd. of 1 Corpl & 6 Privates from Do to Morrow from R. C. Vollinteers.

Detale of the Picketts this Evening.

	C.	S.	S.	D.	R & F.
1st Battn Dulys . . .	o	1	2	1.	30.
3d Battn Do	o	1	1	0.	20.
Md Loyalists	o	1	1	1.	30.
R. C. Volln	1	1	0	0.	20.
Total	1	4	4	2.	100.

Orderly Sergt this Day 1st Battn Dulanceys for to morrow 3d Battn Do The Light Dragoons to Mount a pickett of an Officer & 20 as usuall which are to furnish Patroles for the Camp as usual.

R. O. For the Outline pickett this Night Capt W. Dulaney and Ens Jones—for the Inline Capt Key and Lt. Ingils.

HEAD QUARS MATITUCK AUGt 9th 1778.

Parole, *Farrine*. C Sign

Field Officer for Duty to morrow Lt. Coll. Chalmers Adjt Md Loyalists Gd at Head Quars 1st Battn Dulanys Brigdr Genl. Dulanceys 3d Battn Do.

Detail

Detail for pickets this Evening.

	C.	S.	S.	D.	R. & F.
1ˢᵗ Battⁿ Dulyˢ . . .	0	1	1	0.	30.
3ᵈ Battⁿ Dᵒ	1	2	0	1.	20.
M. Loyalists	1	1	2	0.	30.
R. C. Vollinˢ . . .	0	0	1	1.	20.
Total	2	4	4	2.	100.

Capᵗ Kenlocks Detachment to Take the Cavelry pickett this Evening which will furnish Pattroles to the Camp—

Genl. Tryon has Ofired a Guinney Reward to any Inhabitants of Sauffuck County Who will Apprehend and Bring any Diserter to Camp.

The Commanding Officers of Corps to be Anserable for the Cleanlyness of their Respective Regᵗˢ and Camp and that Proper Nessisariey Houses are made Immediatily. No Horses to wartered at the wells Nor is thier Water to be used from them for washing, there Being a pond on the right of the Camp. That this Order may be puntially fulfilled, sentries from Each Quarˢ to be poasted at the Wells to which the Regts. Drinks warter.

Sergᵗ Antiney Baster of Brigᵈʳ Genˡ Dulanceys Battⁿ is oppointd Assistant provost marshal to the Troops in this Service and to be Observed as Such— A Gᵈ of a Corpral & 6 privates to mount Immediately at the provost Marshals Quarˢ from 3ᵈ Battⁿ Dulanceys

ceys provost g^d to morrow M^d Loyalists—The Genl. Possitively forbids soldiers stragling from Camp and any One of them who is found half a Mile from it will be sent prison^r to the Provost.

R. O. For the outline pickett this night Capt Keys and Lt Ingils—for the Inline Duty Capt Coston and En^s McPherson.

The Commanding Officers Expects that every Company's tents will be properly marked and that the Commanding Officers of Companeys are anserable for the Cleanlyness of their Companeys streets and the Q^r Master for the whole Incampment.

A Reg^{tl} Coart Martial to set Immediately.

Capt Key President.

En^s Jones, } Members. { Lt Ingils,
Lt Townsin, } { Lt Parker.

An Officer of Each Company to be Always in the Regem^{tl} Incampment.

When any of the Officer means to go to the next house or the Reg^{ts} in Camp he is to acquaint the Orderly Serg^t of that Company where he may be found.

No Servants Tents to be seen in the Officers streets. These is to be standing Orders.

R. O. Augt 10th 1778.

A Reg^{tl} Coart Martial to set Immediately.

Capt. Caston President.

En^s McPherson, } Members. { En^s morrow,
Lt Townsin, } { Lt Starling.

Corpl.

Corpl. More of Capt. Wr. Dulaneys Company is Oppointed Sergt. in Capt. Costons Compy. Instead of Sergt. Statton.

HEAD QUARTS MATITUCKETT AUGT. 10TH 1778.

Parole,   C Sign.

Field Officer for Duty tomorrow Major Lynch Adjt. R. C. Volnters Guard at Head Quars. to morrow Md. Loyalists Brigdr. Genl. Dullancys Gd. Do. —Orderly Sergt. 1st. Battn. Dulanceys—Fresh provision to be Isued to the Troops for 4 Days in A Weak untill further orders.

Detale for out pickett this Evening

	C.	S.	S.	D.	R & F.
1st Battn Dulys	1	1	2	1.	32.
3d Battn Do	0	0	1	1.	22.
Md Loyalists	0	2	1	0.	29.
R. C. Volns	1	1	0	0.	17.
Total	2	4	4	2.	100.

Cavelry pickett as useual from Coll. Hameltons— Gen. Tryon has Received Information that Some Disofected Inhabitants on Long Island have by Base and fowl Insinsiation addressed to With Draw the offections of the Soldiers from the Sollom Ingagement they have Entered into to Support the Honner of his Majesteys Crown and Happy Constitution of the County

by

by Incurregeing them to Dissert the Service he hopes
Therefore to Detect all Such Villiness Practise and
Recommend it to Every Soldier who shall be So Dis-
honestly Tampeard with to Shew a proper Indignation
for Such an Insults on his phidilety by approahending
Such Person or Persons and Bringing them to his
Commanding Officer who will Send them to the Pro-
vost that they may be Tryed by a Coart Martial of the
Line.

R. O. For the Outline pickett this Evening En^s
Mc Pherson, and Lieut. Sinclier. For the Inline Duty
Capt. frisby and Lt. Parker.

HEAD QUARS MATITUCK AG^T 11TH 78.

Parole, C. Sign, *Lisly*.

Field Officer for Duty to morrow Lt Coll. Clifton
Adj^t 1st Batt^n Dulanceys—Guard at Head Quar^s 1st
Batt^n D^o Brig^{dr} Genl Dulanys Guard 3^d B^n D^o Or-
derly Serg^t at Head Quar^s 3rd B. D^o provost Guard
M Loyalists. The Corp^l and 8 Men that attended
Major Holland* on the servaying Bisness to attend
Every Morning at Head Qua^{rs} for the Same Pur-
pose till further Orders Without any of them being
Changed.

Detail for the Out Line Pickett This Evening.

---

* Samuel Holland, Surveyor General of the Lands of the Northern
District of America, and Director of the "Guides and Pioneers."

C.

	C.	S.	S.	D.	R & F.
1st Battn Dulys . . .	I	I	I	O.	32.
3d Battn Do	O	2	I	I.	22.
M Loyalists	O	O	I	O.	29.
R C V.	I	I	I	I.	17.
Total	2	4	4	2.	100.

Coll Hameltons Squadren will furnish the Pickets this Evening as Usual.

R. O. For the Out Pickett this Evening Capt G. Dulaney Ens. Monrow.

HEAD QUARS MATITUCK AUGT 12TH 1778.

Parole, *Gray*.   C Sign.

Field Officer for Duty to Morrow Majr Mc Daniald Adjt 3d B Dulanceys guard at Head Quarters Md Loyalists Brigdr Genl Dulanceys Gd 3d B Dulanys Provost Guard Ro. Ca. Vollinteers Orderly Sergt at Head Quars M. Loyalists.

Detale for pickett this Evening.

	C.	S.	S.	D.	R. & F.
1st Battn Dulanceys .	I	I	2	I.	32.
3d Battn Do	I	O	O	O.	22.
M. Loyalists	O	2	2	I.	29.
R. C. Vollinteers . .	O	I	O	O.	17.
Total	2	4	4	2.	100.

Cavelry

Cavelry Pickett from Collinell Hameltons Squadren as Useual.

All Hay, Straw, Corn, and Oats are to be Received for the Commissary of Furrage. All Officers Soldiers and Others Persons are forbid purchising any of those artickels from the Inhabitants without a permitt from the Said Commissarys Obtained for the Quantity Wanted   officers attending Furage viz Genl Field and Staff officers will Receive it from the Commissary of Furrage from the Day they arived into this Camp— Thier Rations to Consist to the 8 Bushals of Oats & no Hay till further Orders. No Quar^s or Stables to be taken unless marked by the Q^r Mas^r Genl—all Horses belonging to Camp are Expected to be kept at Grass or picketed.

A Disobedience of the Above Orders Will be Taken Notice of.

A Corp^l and 6 men to mount to morrow morning on fg^e [?*] Boats at Gerdeen Bensons who are to suffer on no pertence any Boats to go out of the Same without an order from the Qua^r Master Genl —A Corp^l and 6 men will be allso furnished for Cattel Guard. The Qut^r Master Genl will give their Orders—all Inhabitants whose Cattle are Devided on the Kings Service May not withstanding Sell Them to Commissary Genl who has Liberty to With Draw them at his Pleasure. The Qua^r Master Genl Will Allow all

---

* Probably an abbreviation for forage.

Waggons

Waggons Retained in the Kings Service Attending the Command at one Shilling starling Pr Day in Lue of Rations. Cattle Guard to m^w 1st Battn. Dulanceys Guard for the Boats M Loyalists.

R. O. For the Outline Pickett this Evening Lieut. Parker and En^s Monrow—For the Inline Duty Capt. W. Dulaney and Lieu^t Townsand.

HEAD QUAR^s MATITUCK AUG^T 13TH 1778.

Parole *Kingston.*   C Sign, *Nawfolk.*

Field Officer for duty to morrow Major Minsies Adg^t M L G^d at Head Quar^s 1st Batt^n Dulanceys B^{dr} Genl Dulanceys G^d R. C. Voll. Provost 1st Batt^n Dulanceys Cattle Guard M Loyalists G^d for the Sergt. R C Vollinteers.

Detale for outline pickets this Evening.

	C.	S.	S.	D.	R & F.
1st Batt^n Duly^s .	o	1	1	0.	32.
3^d Batt^n D^o . .	o	1	1	1.	22.
M Loyalists . .	1	1	1	1.	29.
R C Vollinteers .	1	1	1	0.	17.
Total . . .	2	4	4	2	100.

Cavelry Pickitt as useual. The Genl. Posatively forbids the Burning of Rails or fences—Commanding Officers will Give to thier Respective Corps Actually as thier Can be Pretence for Such Devistation now that a Plenty a Plenty of Wood is Brought to the Camp for fire. Such Cattle from South Hamton Town ship as are in good Condition the Commissary will Mark for thier use the Armey Two Markett Days in a Weak.

Viz

Wensday and Saterday are Established near the Widdew Hubbord. Soldiers who shall mollist or Interrupt any Persons Comeing or going from the Market will be Sevearly Punished, a Coart marshal of the Line to assemble to morrow morning at 9 O'Clock for the Tryal of all Such prisoners as Shall be Bought before them.

President A Capt. from the 3 B Dulanceys 1 Subbelton from 1st D? 1 Subbelton 3d D? a sub. from the M. Royalists 1 Sub. from the R. C. V. Members.

Detale 1 C 4 Subaltons.

The Prisioners to have the useal Notice the Evidences warned to attend.

Mem. Only such prisioners as are not to be Kept in the Regts Qr Gd will in futer be sent to the Provost.

R. O. For the outline pickett this Evening Capt Frisbey & Lt Townsand—For the Inline Duty Capt Key and Ens Jones.

HEAD QUARS AUGT 14TH 1778.

Parole, *Newport*. C Sign.

Field Officer for Duty to morrow Lieut Colo Cruger.

ger Adj^t. R. C. Vollinteers G^d at Head Q^r 3^d Batt^n Dulanceys B^r Genl Dulanceys. G^d 1st Batt^n D^o Provost G^d M Loyalists Cattle Guard R C Vollinteers. G^d for the Boats M L. Orderly Serg^t 1st Batt^n Dulanceys.

Detail for Out Pickett this Evening.

	C.	S.	S.	D.	R & F.
1st B Dulanceys . 1	1	2	1.	32.
3^d Batt^n D^o . . 1	1	0	0.	22.
M Loyalists . . 0	1	2	1.	29.
R C Vollinteers . 0	1	0	0.	17.
Total . . . 2	4	4	2.	100.

The troops are Acquanted that a Safe Guard is Oppointed to Pertect the Houss in Property of Mr. John Gerden on the Right of the Camp and that who ever Forcable takes Owing [?] anything Under his Carged will be Punished as the Articles of War Dericts in that Cause. The arms And Ammunishon to be Cearfully Examined Every Morning at Troop Beating.

R. O. For the Outline Pickett this Evening En^s Jones. Out Duty Capt Key and En^s Mc Pherson.

The Officers to pitch their Tents Emmediately and Remain in Camp Constantly Agreeable to former Orders. The Commanding Officers of Companeys to see their Companies Tents properly pitched a Return of Tents Wanting to be given in Immediately to the Q^r Master as soon as Possable.

HEAD QUAR^S MATITUCK AUG^T 15TH, 1778.

Parole, *Plemmeth.*   C Sign.

Field Officer for Duty to morrow Major Green
Adj^t * 1st Battⁿ Dulanceys Guard at Head Quar^s M
Loyalists Br^{dr} Genl Dulancey G^d R C Vollinteers
Cattle G^d 1st Battn. Dullanceys Guard for the Boats.
1st Battⁿ D^o Provost G^d 3^d Battⁿ D^o.

Detail for Pickets this Evening.

	C.	S.	S.	D.	R & F.
1st Battⁿ Dullancey	1	1	1	0.	32.
3^d Battⁿ D^o	0	1	1	1.	22.
M Loyalists	1	2	1	0.	29.
R C Vollinteers	0	0	1	1.	17.
Total	2	4	4	2.	100.

Cavelry Picketts from Coll^o Hameltons Squadren.
In Case of an allam in the Night   The inline picket of
1st Battⁿ & 3^d D^o will Repare to Head Quar^s   Those
of the Others two Batt^{ns} will form on the Genl parraid.

R. O.   For the Outline pickett This Evening Capt
Coston and Lt Ingils & En^s M^cpherson.   For the Inline Duty Capt. frisby and Lieu^t Parker.

HEAD QUAR^S MATITUCK AUG^T 16TH, 1778.

Parole, *Luninburg.*   C Sign.

Field Officer for Duty to morrow Lieu^t Col^o Chal-

---

*Joseph Green, Major in Delanceys 1st battalion.

mers

mers Adg.ᵗ 3ᵈ B Dulanceys Gᵈ at Head Qʳˢ Dᵒ Brigᵈʳ
Genˡ Dulanceys Guard 3ᵈ Battⁿ Dᵒ Provost Gᵈ R C
Vo Cattle Gᵈ M L. Guard for the Boats 3ᵈ Dulancys
Orderly Sergᵗ R C Vollinteers.

Detail for Out Pickets this Evening.

	C.	S.	S.	D.	R & F.
1ˢᵗ Battnⁿ Dulyˢ . .	o	1	2	1.	32.
3ᵈ Battⁿ Dᵒ	1	1	o	o.	22.
M Loyalists	1	1	2	1.	29.
R C Vollinteers . .	o	1	o	o.	17.
Total	2	4	4	2.	100.

One Non Commissioned Officer & 10 Privates from
Coll. Hameltons Squadren. A Coart Martial of the
Line to sitt to morrow Morning for the Trial of all
such Prisioners as may be Braught Before them.

President Capᵗ from M Loyalists 1ˢᵗ Battⁿ Dulyˢ,
one Subalton 3ᵈ Battⁿ Dᵒ 1 Subelton M Loyalists 2
Subaltons. The Prisioners to have thier Useual Notice and the Evadences Warned to attend. The Commissary is Derected to Percure from the Inhabitants as
Much flower as Possable and to make a Return of the
Number of Cattle Sent from the Respective Town Ships
in this County—A Sergt. and 12 men the Guard over
the Rebel Privateer to be taken of Immediately.

No Officer to press Herses but the Quarᵗ Mʳ Genˡ
Expects a Return of the Number of women and Children Belonging to Each Corps. to be Given in Immediately.

R. O.

R. O. For the Outline pickett This Evening Capt G. Dulaney and En.^s Starling. for the Inline Duty Capt W. Dulany and En.^s Bowles.

For the Coart Martial of the Line Capt G. Dulaney and Lt Sinclier and En.^s Monrow En.^s McPherson.

for the Q.^r G.^d to morrow Lt Parker.

HEAD QUAR.^S MATITUCK AG.^T 17.TH 1778.

Parole *Durham*. C Sign.

Field Officer for Duty to morrow Major Lynch Adj.^t M L.^s G.^d at Head Q. M. L.; Brig.^{dr} Genl Dulanceys G.^d R C Vollinteers provost G.^d 1.st B Dulanceys Cattle G.^d 3.rd Batt.ⁿ D.^o G.^d for the Boats M Loyalists Orderly Serg.^t 1.st Batt.ⁿ Dulanceys—Provost Guard in futer to Consist of a Serg.^t a Corp.^l and 9 privates

Detail for Outline picketts this Evening.

	C.	S.	S.	D.	R & F.
1.st Batt.ⁿ Dulanceys .	1	1	1	0.	32.
3.^d B D.^o .	0	1	1	1.	22.
M Loyalists	0	1	1	0.	29.
R C Vollinteer . . .	1	1	1	1.	17.
Total	2	4	4	2.	100.

Cavelry Pickett from Capt. Kenlocks Light Dragoons—Mr. Daniald Ozbern, Selvester Lesister are Oppointed Commissaryes for Vitualing The Extrey Waggons Imployed by the Genl Order.

The

The Qr. Mr. Genl. will make a Return Every morning of the Number Retained which will be for the said Commissaries Devotier. The Q^r Mr Genl will make a Return Every morning of the Number Retained which will be for the said Commissaries Devotier. The Q^r Master Genl to Give in a Return of Oxen and Teams Retain^d for the Importing the Commissaryes Stores & the Oxen to be Constantly kept to geather and not Seperated The Cattle Guard is March with them Breake of Day Every Morning to the Best Pasture, Those two or three Miles from Camp and Return with them in the Evening. Dureing the Night they are to be kept in the Swamp on the Right of the Camp— The Drivers are not to Leave their Quarters without the Q^r Mas^r Genl Permition That the whole may be Ready to march at the shortest Notice. No Provision to be Drawn for Either Women or Children not preasent with the Camp—who are to be shown to the Commissary to morrow morning at OClock in the Rare of the Severall Corps Distinguishing womin from Children and will wait on those Officer who have families for their Names and No.

R. O. For the Outline pickett this Night Lieut Sinclier. for the Inline Duty Capt Key and En^s Monrow. For the Qr. Guard to morrow En^s Bowles.

HEAD QUAR^S MATITUCK AUG^T 18TH 1778.

Parole, *Eddinburgh*.　　　　　C Sign.

Field Officer for Duty to m^w Lieut. Colo. Clifton adj^t R C Voln. guard at head Quar^s 1st Batt^n Dulanceys B^dr Gen Dulanceys G^d 3^d Batt^n D^o Cattle G^d R C Volinters G^d for the Boats D^o Orderly Serg^t 3^d B Dulanceys

Detail for outline pickett this Evg

	C.	S.	S.	D.	R & F.
1st Batt^n Dulanceys . o	1	2	1.	32.
3^d Batt^n D^o . . . . o	1	o	o.	22.
M Loyalists 1	2	2	1.	29.
R C Vollin^s 1	o	o	o.	17.
Total 2	4	4	2.	100.

Cavelry pickett Millitia Light Dragoons—A Return of Carpenters and Black Smiths to be Given to Day from Each Corps—The Commissary Appointed for the Extrey Waggons are to Victual the Countrey confind [?] in the provost The Persist [?] Martials Return will be thier porshon.

R. O. For the outline pickett this Evening Capt W Dulaney Lieu^t Townsin & En^s Morrow—For the Inline Duty Capt Coston and En^s Jones. Q^r G^d to morrow Morning En^s Jones.

HEAD QUAR^S MATITUCK AUG^T 19TH 78.

Field Officer for Duty to morrow Major McDaniald

adg^t.

adg^t 1st Batt^n Dulanceys G^d at head Quar^s 3^d Batt^n
D^o Brig^d Genl. Dulanceys. G^d R C Vollinteers Pro-
vost G^d M L—Cattle and Boat Guard 1st Batt^n Duly^s
Orderly Serg^t R C Vollinteers.

Detail for Outline picketts this Evening.

	C.	S.	S.	D.	R & F.
1st Battn^n Dulancys .	1	1	2	1.	32.
3^d Batt^n D^o	1	1	1	0.	22.
M^d Loyalists . . .	0	1	1	1.	29.
R C Vollns	0	1	0	0.	17.
Total	2	4	4	2	100.

Cavelry pickett Militia Light Dragoons who are in
futer to perrade at their Own Quar^s an Houre before
sun sett and March from thence to their poasts without going to the Genl. Parade and they will Report to
the Field Offic^r of the Day.

R. O. For the Out pickett this Evening Lieu^t Ingils for the Inline Duty Capt G. Dulaney & En^s M^c-
pherson.

HEAD QUAR^s MATITUCK AUG^T 20TH, 1778.

Parole, *Cathcart.*   C S *Rawdon.*

Field Officer for Duty to morrow Col^o Huwlitt
Adg^t 3^d Batt^n D^{ys} Guard at Head Quar^s R C Vollin^s
Brig^d Genl. Dulanceys G^d 3^d B Dulancey Provost
G^d 1st Batt^n D^o Cattle and Boat G^d M Loyalists Or-
derly Serg^t 1st Batt^n Dulancys.

Detail

Detail for Outline pickets this Evening.

	C.	S.	S.	D.	R. & F.
1ˢᵗ Battⁿ Dulancys .	1	1	1	1.	32.
2ᵈ Battⁿ Do	0	1	1	0.	22.
Mᵈ Loyalists	0	1	1	1.	29.
R C Vollinteers . .	1	1	1	0.	17.
Total	2	4	4	2.	100.

Cavelry pickett Capᵗ Kinlock Light Dragoons.

The Sentance of the Coart Martial of the Line of Capt. G. Dulaney was prisident will be put in Execution this Evening at 5 O'Clock On the Grand Perrade when the Troops will be Ordered Under arms for that Purpose. A Sergien to Attend. The Commissary to Deliver the Kings Allowance of Rum to the Troops. To pertect fals Allarms No Officer or Soldier is Permitted to Discharge fire arms in the Neighborhood or the Camp.

R. O. For the Out Duty this Evening Ens. Sterling. for the Inline Duty Capᵗ W. Dulaney & Lieuᵗ Sinclier. Quarˢ Guard to Morrow Lieut. Sterling.

HEAD QUARˢ MATITUCK. AUGᵀ 21ˢᵀ, 1778.

Parole.   C Sign.

Field Officer for Duty to morrow Major Minzen [Menzies] Adgᵗ M Loyalists Gᵈ at Head Quaʳˢ M L Gᵈ at Genˡ Dulanceys Quarˢ 1ˢᵗ Battⁿ Dulanceys

Provost

Provost 3ᵈ Battⁿ Dᵒ Cattle Gᵈ Dᵒ Gᵈ for the Boats R
C Vollinteers Orderly Sergᵗ 3ᵈ Battⁿ Dulanceys
Detail for pickett this Evening.

	C.	S.	S.	D.	R & F.
1ˢᵗ Battⁿ Dulancys . 1	1	1	O.	32.
3ᵈ Battⁿ Dᵒ . . . . O	1	1	1.	22.
M Loyalists 1	1	1	O.	29.
R C Volns. . . . . O	1	1	1.	17.
Total 2	4	4	2.	100.

Cavelry pickett Militia Light Dragoons. An Officers an 20 of the Out Pickets in the Rare of Hᵈ Quarˢ.

R. O. For the Outline Duty this Evening Capᵗ
Jones and Enˢ Bowls. for Inline Duty Capᵗ Key and
Lᵗ Parker. Quartʳ Gᵈ to morrow Lieuᵗ Parker.

Genl Orders.

The men whose names are on the Other side are to
be perraded at 2 O'Clock this Afternoon With 4 Days
provision and Rum they are to be under the Command
of Capt. Coffin of the Whale Boats.

After Orders 21ˢᵗ —

The 3ᵈ Battⁿ Dulancys to march to Morrow morning.

They will Detatch an Officer and 20 men with the
Teames at 5 O'Clock and Receive the provision from
board the ships—The Qʳ Masʳ Genˡ will show the
Battⁿ the Ground on which they are to In Camp on—

Colo.

Colo. Ludloe* will Order Such Guard for the security of his Camp and provision as he should think Nessary.

HEAD QUAR^S MATITUCK AUG^T 22^D 1778.

Parole,   C Sign.

Field Officer for Duty this Day Colo. Cruger for to morrow Major Green adg^t R C Vollin^s Guard at Head Qr^s 1st Battⁿ Dulany^s Brigd^r Genl Dulanceys G^d R C Volⁿ provost G^d to morrow M^d Loyalists Cattle G^d D^o Boat Guard of a Corp^l & 3 men 1st Battⁿ Dulanceys.   Orderly Serg^t this Day M Loyalists to morrow R C Vollinteers.

Detail for out Pickets this Evening.

	C.	S.	S.	D.	R & F.
1st Battⁿ Duly^s . . .	0	1	2	1.	30.
M Loyalists	1	2	1	1.	30.
R C Vollinteers . .	1	1	1	0.	20.
Total	2	4	4	2.	80.

Cavelry pickett Melitia Light Dragons.

R. O.   For the outline Duty this evening Capt Key Lt Sterling and En^s Jones for the Inline Duty Capt Frisby and Lt Townsin Quar. Gd. to morrow Lt. Townsin.

---

* Gabriel Ludlow of Long Island, commander of Dulancey's 3d Battalion. See *Sabine*, II, 34. His estate was declared forfeited by the act of Oct. 22, 1779, and this forfeiture was confirmed by the act of May 12, 1784.

HEAD QUAR^s MATITUCK AUG^T 23^D 1778.

Parole, C Sign.

Field Officer for Duty to morrow Lieut. Col^o Chalmers Adg^t. 1st B Dullanceys Guard at head Quar^s M Loyalists Brig^{dr} Genl. Dully^s Guard 1st Battⁿ D^o Provost Guard D^o Cattle and Boat G^d R C Vollinters. Orderly Serg^t 1st Battⁿ Dulanceys.

Detail for Outline pickett this Evening.

	C.	S.	S.	D.	R & F.
1st Battⁿ Dulany^s . .	1	2	1	1.	30.
M Loyalists	0	1	2	1.	30.
R C Vollinteers . .	1	1	1	0.	20.
Total	2	4	4	2.	80.

Cavelry pickett Capt. Kenlocks Troops.

Officers are not to press or hire Horses of the Inhabitants without Permission for which they are in All Immaginations to apply at Head Quar^s or the Quar^r Mast^r Genl where they will obtain it.

R. O. For the Outline Duty this Night Lieut Ingils. for the Inline Duty Capt. Coston En^s McPherson Q^r G^d to morrow En^s McPherson.

HEAD QUARS^s MATITUCK AUG^T 24th, 1778.

Parrole, C Sign.

Field Officer for Duty to m^w Major Lynch adg^t M Loyalists G^d at Head Quar^s 1st Battⁿ Dulanc^{ys} Brigd^r Genl.

Genl Dulanceys M Loyalists provost G^d R C Vollinteers, Cattle Guard M L. Boat G^d 1st Batt^n Dulanceys
Orderly Serg^t M Loyalists.

Detail for out Line pickett this Evening.

	C.	S.	S.	D.	R & F.
1st Batt^n Dulancys .	I	I	2	I.	31.
M Loyalists	I	2	I	I.	29.
R C Vollin^s	0	I	I	0.	20.
Total	2	4	4	2.	80.

Cavelry pickett Militia Light Dragons. The Troops
to hold them Selves in Readiness to March at the
Shortest Notice.

R. O. For the Outline Duty this Evening Capt
Key and En^s Sterling & Lt Sinclier for the Inline
Duty Capt Jones and En^s Bowles Q^r G^d En^s Bowles.

After Orders 4 O'Clock. 24th Augt 1778.

The troops to March to Morrow morning at 6
O'Clock one Days Provision to be Immediately De-
liver^d to the Troops which must be cook this Evening.

HEAD QUAR^s WAIDEN RIVER* AUG^T 25TH 1778.

Parole,

Field Officer for Duty to morrow Lieu^t Col^o Clifton adg^t R C Voll^{rs} G^d at Head Quar^s D^o Brig^{dr}
Genl Dulanceys G^d 1st Batt^n D^o provost G^d M Loyal-

---

* Probably intended for Wading River, in Riverhead Township, L. I.

ists

ists Cattle 1ˢᵗ Battⁿ Dulanceys—Provision Guard M
Loyalists Orderly Sergᵗ 1ˢᵗ Battⁿ Dulanceys Guard
Ordered Yesterday ye Total to Mount Immediately.
Detail for out pickett this Evening.

	C.	S.	S.	D.	R & F.
1ˢᵗ Battⁿ Dullyˢ . .	0	0	2	1.	19.
M L	0	1	1	0.	18.
R C Vollinteers . .	1	1	0	0.	13.
Total	1	2	3	1.	50.

On Account of the Great heat of The Day and the
Driness of the march The Genˡ. has thought proper
to Order Each man A Guill of Rum which the Officers
are Desired to see it Mixed with a Proportion of
Water—The troops to March to Morrow Morning at
5 O'Clock. The Line to move of from the Right
Colo. Hameltons Squaⁿ to form the advance Guard
Capt. Kenlocks the Rare who will furnish a Corpˡ. and
4 for the Cattle Guard.

HEAD QUARˢ. MILLERS PLACE,* AUGᵀ 26ᵀᴴ, 1778.

Parole,   C Sign.

Field Officer for Duty to morrow Major MᶜDaniald
adjᵗ. 1ˢᵗ Battⁿ Dulanceys Brigᵈʳ Genˡˢ Guard R C
Vollinteers. Guard at Head Quarˢ. M L provost
Guard the 1ˢᵗ Battⁿ Dulanceys Cattle Gᵈ R C V pro-

* In Brookhaven township, L. I.

vision

vision Guard of a Serg^t a Corp^l and 9 men from 1st Batt^n Dulanceys Orderly Serg^t M : Loyalists. Orderly Serg^t for the Adg^t Genl this Day 1st Batt^n Dulanceys for tom^w R C Vollinteers.

Detail for the pickett this Evening.

	C.	S.	S.	D.	R & file.
1st Batt^n Duly^s . . .	1	1	1	0.	19.
M Loyalists	0	1	1	1.	18.
R C Vollinteers . .	0	0	1	0.	13.
Total	1	2	3	1.	50.

Cavelry pickett from Capt. Kenlocks of a Corp^l and 4 who is to pattrol the Beach to the Eastward of the Camp. The fences are not to be Burnt or Distroyed. The Q^r Mast^r Genl will order the Inhabitants to Carry fuel to the Camps for the Nessary use thereof Immediately.

R. O. For the Outline Duty this Evening En^s Jones. Inline Duty Lieut. Townsin Quar^r G^d to Morrow Lt Townsin Capt for the Day Capt W. Dulaney.

HEAD QUAR^s MILLERS PLACE AUG^T 27, 78.

Parrole,   C Sign.

Field Officer for Duty to morrow Lt Col^o Cruger adj^t M Loyalists Guard at Head Quars. 1st Batt^n Dulancys. Brig^{dr} Genl Dulanceys G^d 3^d Batt^n D^o Provost G^d M Loyalists Cattle G^d 3^d Batt^n Dulanceys

provision

provision G^d R C Vollinteer. Orderly Sergt. 3d.
Battn. Dulanceys.

Detail for Out Pickett this Evening.

	C.	S.	S.	D.	R & F.
1st Battn. Dullys. . .	o	1	1	o.	19.
M. Loyalists	1	o	2	1.	18.
R. C. Vollinteers . .	o	1	o	o.	13.
Total	1	2	3	1.	50.

Cavelry pickett Militia Light Dragoons—The
Troops. to March to morrow morning at 4 O'Clock.
The Order of the March the Same as from Waiden
River Excepting Capt. Kenlocks to form the Vance
Guard and Colo. Hameltons the Rare Gd. The Teams
and Waggons to be in Readiness to Move with the
Troops.

R. O. For the Out Line Duty this Evening Capt.
G. Dulaney—for the Inline Duty Capt. Keys L^t. Ingils
to morrow Before the troops march off.

HEAD QUAR^S. SATUCKETT AUG^T. 28TH.

Parole,   C Sign.

Field Offi^r. for Duty to morrow Major Green Adj^t.
R C Vollinter G^d at Head Quar^s. M^d Loyalists Brig^dr
Genl. Dulanceys this Day M Loyalists to morrow 1st
Batt^n Duly^s provost G^d R C V provision G^d 1st Batt^n
Dulanceys Cattle G^d. this Day R C V to morrow M
                                      Loyalists

Loyalists Orderly Serg^t this Day M Loyalists to morrow Ist Batt^n Dulanceys.

Detail for Out Pickett this Ev^{ng}.

	C.	S.	S.	D.	R & F.
Ist Batt^n Dulancys .	2	0	2	I.	24.
M Loyalists	0	2	I	0.	21.
R C Vollinteers . . .	0	I	0	0.	15.
Total	I	3	3	I.	60.

Cavelry pickett of a Corp^l and 6 from Militia Light Dragoons. The 3^d Batt^n Dulanceys to march to morrow at I–C^k this Day the Rest to hold them Selves in Readiness to march to morrow.

R. O. For the Outline picket En^s M^{c}pherson & En^s Sterling for this Day Capt frisby Q^r G^d to morrow Lieut. Sinclier.

HEAD QUARS. SATUCKITT AUGT. 29TH, 78.

Parole,   C Sign.

Field Officer for Duty to morrow Lieut. Col^o Chalmers Adj^t Ist Batt^n Dulanceys G^d at Head Quar^s D^o Brigd^r Genl. Dulanceys. G^d 3^d Batt^n Dulanceys Orderly Serg^t R C V.

Detail for Out pickett this Evening.

	C.	S.	S.	D.	R & F.
Ist Batt^n Dulanceys .	I	I	2	I.	24.
R C Vollinteers . . .	0	I	0	0.	16.
Total	I	2	2	I.	40.

The

The First Battⁿ Dulanceys with the field peices and the Detatchmᵗ of Colᵒ Hameltons to march this Day at 12 O'Clock—Capt. Hewlett with the Remainder of Militia Light Dragoons to Escort the Cattle he will Receive Orders Derectt from Colo. Hamelton. A Corpˡ and 4 Light Dragoons from Capᵗ Kenlocks to parrade Emmediately to Escort Mr. Cutler* Assistant Commissary to the Eastward. The Corpˡ will Receive Derictions from Mr. Cutler.

R. O. For the Out Line Duty Capᵗ Jones Lieuᵗ Parker—for the Day Capᵗ G. Dulaney Qʳ Gᵈ to morrow Enˢ Bowls.

After Orders 29 Augt. 1778.

Devine Service will be performed at 8 O'Clock to morrow morning and the Troops to March at 9.

Head Quars. Smyth Town.   Augt. 30th, 1778.

Parrole,   C Sign.

Field Officer for Duty to Morrow Major Lynch adjᵗ M Loyalists Gᵈ at Head Quarˢ the Detachment of that was Left with the provision Gᵈ M L at Brigᵈ Genˡ Dulanceys Dᵒ provost Gᵈ R C Voln. Orderly Sergᵗ M Loyalists.

Detail for out Pickett this Evening.

---

* John Cutler, " collector of forage and horses at Long Island," under Daniel Weir, Commissary General.

C.

	C.	S.	S.	D.	R & F.
M Loyalists	o	2	1	1.	24.
R C Vollonteers . .	1	o	1	o.	16.
Total	1	2	2	1	40.

Patroles from the Q^r of Militia Light Dragoons to Head Q^r During the Night—D^o from Capt. Kenlocks on the Road in the Rare of head Q^rs

R. O. For the Outline Duty Lt Sterling and En^s Jones for the Day Capt. Jone^s Q^r G^d Lt Townsin.

MORNING ORDERS AUGT. 31ST, 1778.

Regeam^t Coart Martial to Sett Immediately Capt. Jones. President.

En^s Jones,
Lieu^t Ingils, } Members. { Lt Sinclier,
En^s Sterling.

HEAD QUAR^s SMYTHS TOWN. AUG^T 31ST 1778.

Parole,   C Sign.

Field Officer for Duty to m^w Lieu^t Col^o Clifton adj^t R C V G^d at Head Q^r M Loyalists provision G^d R C Vollonteers. Provost 3^d Batt^n Dulanceys Orderly Serg^t R C Vollinteers.

Detale for pickett this Evening.

C.

	C.	S.	S.	D.	R & F.
M L	1	1	2	1.	24.
R C Vo	0	1	0	0.	16.
Total	1	2	2	1.	40.

Cavelry pickett as Last Night. The Troops to hold them Selves In Readiness to March.

R. O. For the Out pickett this Evening Capt Ingils for the Day Capt Key for the Q^r G^d En^s Mcpherson. Corp^l Merrill of Capt Jones Company is Oppoynted Serg^t and Obediah Smyth Oppointed Corp^l

After Orders 6 OClock.

The Troops to march to morrow at 6 OClock Leaving an Officer and 30 men of M Loyalists to Escort the Cattle the Officer will Receive Orders from Colo. Willit* Commissary for the Same—En^s Sterling for the Above Duty.

HEAD QUARS. HUNTINGTON, SEP^T 1ST, 1778.

Parrole,   C Sign.

Field Officer for Duty to morrow Major McDaniald adj^t 1st Batt^n Dulanceys G^d at Head Quar^s 1st Batt^n D^o Brig^{dr} Genl Dulanceys G. 3^d Batt^n D^o Provision G^d M Loyalists provost G^d R C Vollonteers. Orderly Serg^t 1 Batt^n Dulanceys The two Batt^n Dulancey with the field peices to March to morrow at 5 OClock

---

* Halijah Willard, "Commissary of Cattle at New York."

and

and in Camp at Witberry till further Orders. The Remaindin Battⁿ with Capt Kenlocks to hold them-Selves in Readiness to march when Ordered—The Remaindin Detatchment of Coll. Hameltons has the Gen^{ls} Permission to Return Home who Desires Coll. Hamelton to take the first Oppertunety of Giveing to the Respective Troops his perticular thanks for thier Regular Behavour on this Service.

An Out pickett of an Officer and 30 men from the two Battⁿ to Mount on the Right this Evening.

	C.	S.	S.	D.	R & F.
1st Battⁿ Du^{lys} . . .	0	1	1	0.	18.
3^d Battⁿ D^o	0	0	0	0.	30.
Total	0	1	1	0.	30.

R. O. For the Day Capt W. Dulany for the Q^r Guard Lieut. Sinclier.

A Reg^{tl} Coart Martial to Sett Immediately.

Capt W Dulaney Prisident.

Ens Bowls, }
Lt Parker, } Members. { Lt Sterling,
{ Ens Monrow.

HEAD QUARS HUNTINGTON SEPT 2D, 78.

Parole,   C Sign.

Field Officer for Duty to Morrow Lieut Colo Hulett adjt 3d B Dulanceys Gd at Head Quars M L to morrow 1st Battn Dulancey's provision R C Vollinteers

teers provost G^d M L orderly Sergt M L to morrow
1st Batt^n Dulanceys.   Detail for pickett this Evening.

	C.	S.	S.	D.	R & F.
M L	o	1	1	o.	18.
R C V	1	o	o	o.	12.
Total	1	1	1	o.	30.

The Troops to March to Morrow Morning at 4
OClock. Two Days Provision to Be Isued to them
Immediately which must be Cookd as Soon as Re-
ceived.

R. O. For the Out Pickett this Evening. En^s
Bowles. for the Q^r G^d Lieu^t Parker for the Day Capt
Frisby.

HEAD QUARS.   WITBERRY SEP^T 3^D, 1778.

Parole, *Ludlow.*   C. Sign, *Cruger.*

Field Officer for Duty to morrow Lt Col^o Cruger
adj^t M Loyalists Brigd^r Genl Dullanceys G^d this
Day 1st Batt^n Dulanceys to m^w 3^d Batt^n D^o provost
G^d this Day 3^d Batt^n D^o Provision M L Orderly
Serg^t 1st Batt^n Dulanceys.

Sir Henry Clinton has been pleased to Signify his
pleasure that Such Fresh Provision which in Lieu^t
Col^o Cliftons R C Volln. as are Desireus to Serve with
Lord Rawdon in the Vollinteer of Ireland have his
Excellincys Leave to join Lord Rawden and are to
be Delivered to Lieut. Colo. [Welbore E.] Doyle the

100

100 suits of Cloathing Sent to Camp for Lieut. Coll. Chalmers and Lieut Colo. Cliftons Batt^ns will be Delivered Betwen those Corps the Respective Quar^s Mast^rs Giveing Recepts to the Inspecter Genl of Provincial forces for the Same—The Commander in Chief has Derect^d that Brig^dr Genl Dulancey take command of the Troops now under the command of Genl Tryon who will march and Incamp on the Most Conveniantest Ground at Flushinfly and Waite there till further Orders from Lieut. Genl Cornwallis.

M: Brigade Waller to Retain with these Corps till further Orders The Eight Extrey Waggons taken up for Transporting the Commissarys provisions to be Dismist at Flushin Fly? The Q^r Mr Genl giveing Recepts for the Time they have Been Imployd Respective by. Genl Tryon Cannott Quitt his Command without Returning his best Acknowligement to both offi^rs and Soldiers for their C[h]earfulness which they Supported the Heate and phertuage of Long Marches at the Same Time He must Express the Great uneasness he has from the Frequent Disertion* among

---

* "We are informed that General Tryon, with a detachment of troops from New York, has lately been on the East end of Long Island, plundering and driving off all the cattle in that quarter; and that in this excursion he had lost a great number of his men by disertion; who, after they had deser.ed, hid themselves in woods and bye places, in order to embrace every opportunity in coming over to the Main, which had been greatly facilitated by our people sending boats over for that purpose."—*N. J. Gazette, Aug. 26, 1778.*

Some

Some of the Troops which he is Persuaded is arrove from an anxious Desire to See thier absent Fameleys and [not?] Disaffection he therefore Recomends to the Soldiers a patiant to perceive are [persevere?] in their Duty which will Intitle them to honor and fame [?] in the field and Hapiness with thier famelyes whene his Majusty Shall no farther Nead of thier Volintears Service The Genl. Returns his thanks allso Capt. Kenlocks and the Troops under his Command for thier Active and Reguler Behaver The Above Orders to be Read By an Officer at the Head of Each Comp^ny

Brig^dr Genl. Dulanceys Orders.

The 3^d Batt^n D^o to March Immediaty and Encamp at Flushing Fly The Quar^r. Mast^r. Genl. will Show them their Ground. The M Loyalists and R C Vollinteers will march to morrow morning at 4 O'Clock.

In the Same pors^t. The Strictest Dessapline to be Obtained on the March.

R. O. For the Day Capt. Coston Q^r. G^d to morrow En^s. Monrow.

Genl. Court Martial held on fryday Capt. Jones Capt. Key and Lieu^t. Sinclier.

Head Quar^s. Flushing Fly Sep^t. 4th 1778.

Parole, *Vaughn.* C Sign.

Field Officer for Duty to morrow Major Green adj^t

R. C.

R C Vollinteers Brig^dr Genl. Dulancys G M˙ Loyalists Provost G^d of a Serg^t. and 12 men from R C Vollinteers. Orderly Serg^t. 3^d Batt^n Dulanceys.

The Genl. Expects The Commanding Officers of Corps will use thier utmost Exertion to Pertect the Property of the Inhabitants and not Suffer the Cornfields Orcherds gardens or fences to be Distroyed or Damaged without Sevearly punishing the offinder Each Corps to Send to the provost for thier prisioners and Confine them in their Respective Q^r. Guards. The field Officer of the Dày to Order the Rounds and Pattroles and Receive the Reports of the picketts as useual—which he will Report accordingly. The soldiers not to be Allowed to Stray from the Incampment, and if any are found 1 Mile from Camp without a Ritten Pass Signed by an Officer They will Be taken up and Deamed as Disserted No Officer to Lay out of the Camp without the Genl. Permission The Genl Coart Martial to assemble to Morrow Morning in the Camp at Such place as Col^o Ludlow Shall think Proper.

R. O. For the Day Capt. G. Dulaney for the Inline pickett this Evening Lieu^t. Sterling allso for the Q^r. Guard to Morrow.

HEAD QUARS. FLUSHING FLY SEP^T. 5 78.

Parole, C Sign.

Field Officer for Duty to Morrow Lieut. Col^o Chalmers

mers Adj^t 1st Batt^n Dulancys Brig^{dr} Genl Dulancys
Guard 1st Batt^n D^o Orderly Serg^t M Loyalists the
soldiers are not to pay more than 6 pence p^r Quart
for milk.

R. O. For the Day Capt. Jones. For the Inline
pickett and Q^r Guard to morrow En^s Jones—the Officers and Companies to Receive thier mens arms and
Acutrements and Nessaryes to morrow morning and
Give in a Return of what may be Wanting. They are
to make up thier Mens Accounts as Soon as Possable
that the men may be Settled and payed off.

HEAD QUAR^s FLUSHING FLY SEP^T 6TH 1778.

Field Officer for Duty to morrow Major Lynch
adj^t. 3^d Batt^n Dul^{ys} Guard at Genl Dulanceys L. A.
Reg^t provost G^d M. Loyalists Orderly Serg^t R C
Vollinteers.

R. O. For the Day Capt. frisby Inline pickett and
Q^r G^d Lt Ingils.

HEAD QUAR^s FLUSHING FLY SEP^T 7TH 1778.

Parole. C Sign.

Field Officer for Duty to Morrow Lieu^t Col^o Clifton adj^t. L A. Reg^t G^d at Genl Dulanceys Quar^s 3^d
Batt^n Dulanceys. provost G^d R C Vollinteers. Orderly Serg^t 1st Batt^n Dulanceys

R. O.

R. O. For the Day Capt. Coston Inline pickett and
Q^r G^d to Morrow En^s McPherson.

HEAD QUAR^s FLUSHING FLY. SEP^T 8TH 1778.

Field Officer for Duty to Morrow Major McDaniald
adj^t M L Gd at Head Q^r M Loyalists Provost G^d
1st Batt^n Dulancys Orderly Sergt. 3^d Batt^n D^o.

R. O. For the Day to Morrow to Mount at Troops
Beating Capt. Kennedy. Inline pickett and Q^r G^d Lieu^t
Parker Officer of the Guard.

To Search all the Tents and Hutts Round the Camp
and take Prisioners Such as have Sperrits for Sale—
and Secure thier Licquer. The Capt. of the Day to
Visseat the Hospittals and Report whatt he finds amiss
they are to See that the Encampment from the G^d to
the Rare of the Officer Tents is Swept Clean the tents
Properly pitched and the arms Neatly Sett up he
Should Vissit the Guards early in the Night. Exam-
mine the Sentreys that they have thier proper posts
and Order Derect. The Pattroles for the Night & See
That the Fires and Lights are putt out The People in
thier Tents and Hutts Round as well as In Camp are
at Rest he Should Before Day Light Vissitt the G^{ds}
Gitt them under arms and not Suffer them to Sett
Down Lay till Revalley has Beat. any Thing amiss
with respect to the Batt^n Should Be Reported to the
Commanding Officers of the Reg^t as that of the Duty
of the Field Officers of the Day.

Head Quar^s Flushing Fly, Sep^t 9th, 1778.
Parole.

Field Officer for Duty to morrow Lt Col^o Cruger
adj^t R C Volln. G^d at Genl Dullanceys Q^r 1st Battⁿ
Dullanceys provost G^d Loyall A M Reg^t.

R O   For the Day to morrow Capt. Frisby Pickett
& Q^r Guard to morrow En^s M^cpherson.

Sept. 10th, 1778.

The Spear [spare] arms and Cloathing to be Sent to
the Store at Brooklyn by the Waggons to morrow
morning The Officers will Observe that on a march for
the Futur they are to have Only three Waggons for
the 7 Companeys and therefore had Better nott En-
craise their Baggage.

Head Quar^s Flushing fly Sep^t 10th 1778.
Parrole.

Fueld Officer for Duty to mor^w Major Green adj^t
1st Battⁿ Du^{lys} Guard at Genl Dulanceys Q^{rs} L A M
Reg^t Orderly Serg^t M Loyalists.

R. O.   The Officer of the Old Guard to Give a far-
well Report of the New with all Prisioners & Names
and Respective Companies & by whom Confined punishment Inflicted to geather with a Detail of the Guard
N^o of Sentries by Day and Night Another of the Same
form is to be Delivered as Soon as Relevved adding
the Parole & C Sign.

HEAD QUARS. FLUSHING FLY SEP? 11ᵀᴴ 1778.

Parole. C. Sign.

Field Officer for Duty to morᵂ Lᵗ Colᵒ Robertson adjᵗ 3ᵈ Battⁿ Dulanceys Gᵈ at Genˡ Dulanceys Qʳ 3ᵈ Dᵒ provost Gᵈ Dᵒ 1ˢᵗ B Dulanceys Orderly Sergᵗ Dᵒ

Genˡ Tryon having Directed That 100 & 10 Guinneys of the Money arrising from the fines Leavied by the Court Martial of the Line at Matituck Should be Distributed in the following proportions to the Commandin Officers of thier Corps—For the Bennifitt of the Womin and Children They are therefore Requested to Call on M. Brigᵈᵉ Waller for the Same to morrow at 10 O'Clock

Genl Tryons Distribulation

The 1ˢᵗ Battⁿ Dulancys . . . . . 20 Guinneys.
" 3ᵈ Battⁿ Dᵒ . . . . 20 Dᵒ
M Loyalists . . . . 20 Dᵒ
R C Vollinteers . . . . . . 20 Dᵒ
Capt. Kenlocks . . . . 10 Dᵒ
Kings Loyall A Regt. . . . . 10 Dᵒ
Prince of whales* L. A. Voll. . 10 Dᵒ

Total . . . . 110 Dᵒ

All Officers Soldiers or Inhabitants are forbid Dischargeing of fire arms Either in the Neighbourhood or Camp.

---

* The Prince of Wales Volunteers, commanded by Colonel, afterwards Brigadier General Mountfort Brown. See Onderdonk's *Revolutionary Incidents of Queens County*, 142.

R. O.

R. O. For the Day to Morrow Capt. Kennedy
pickett Q^r. G^d. En^s. Jones.

HEAD QUAR^s. FLUSHING FLY SEP^T. 12TH, 1778.
Parole,   C. Sign.
Field Officers for Duty to morow Major Barclay*
adj^t. L. A. Regt. Genl. Dulanceys G^d. 1st Batt^n. Dulancys provost G^d. M Loya^l. Orderly Serg^t. 3^d. Batt^n. Dulanceys.
R. O. For the Day to Morrow Capt. W Dulaney
pickett and Quar^r. G^d. Lieut. Townsin.

HEAD QUAR^s. FLUSHING FLY SEP^T. 13TH. 1778.
Parole,   C Sign.
Orders the Commanding in Chieff has been pleased
to Make the following permotions ye 27th Reg^t. Lieut.
Richards Norriss From ye 17th of foot to be Capt. by
Perchuse Vice Burley who Retired the 10th Sep^t. 45
Reg^t. Charles Inniss to be En^s. by purchase Vice
Rafters Disseased the 30th of May 1778 The Pur-
chase money to be Imployed in bying the adj^t.ancy
and Sergt. Major Darkins as a Reward for the faithfull
Service—Sergt. Major Darkins to be Adj^t. Vice Tayler
by purchase 11th Sept. 1778 34th Regt. Lt. John
More to be Capt. by Perchase Vice Tydwell who Re-
tired the 2d December 1778—Prisioners Tryed by the

---

* Thomas Barclay of the Loyal American Regiment.

Genl.

Genl. Court Martial of which Lieut. Colo [Ralph]
Abercromby was Prisident John Monk Waggoner
in the Q^r Mr Gen^{ls} Department Tryed for Stealing
Severrall pieces of Broad Cloath Blanketts & when
posted to take Cear [care] of Said articles is Found
Guilty and Sentanced to Receive 1000 Lashes John
Connelly private Soldier in the 64th Battⁿ Tryed for
having Disserted from said Reg^t is found Guilty and
Sentanced to Receive 1000 Lashes—John Morgan
Serg^t of Ship Genl Vaine is Tryed for Plundering is
found Not Guilty and Therefore Acquited John
Nathersall Mate James Creaton Gunner and Thomas
Arrowlin Carpenter of the Said ship Genl. Vaun Tryed
For plundering and Secreting his Majesty stores and
Doth therefore adjudge him John Nathersall to Re-
ceive 500 Lashes and then to be sent to service on
Board his Majestys Navy—James Creton and Thomas
Arrolin to Receive 100 hundred Lashes Each and to
be sent to Service on Board his Majestys Navey—The
Coart is of the opinion that they are not Guilty of
Plundering and therefore acquite them of the Same.
Peter Brown private Soldier of the M Loyalists Tryed
for Dissertion and found Guilty and Sentanced to Re-
ceive 500 Lashes. The Commander in Chief approves
of the Above Senta^{ce} Prisioners Tryed By the Genl.
Court Martial of which Lieut. Col^o Clark* was prisident Viz. to Lieut James Ryder Mowatt of the 38th

---

*Alured Clarke.

Regt.

Reg.^t of foot Tryed for staying Out of New York without Leave and Saying before a Reg.^t Court Martial that he had his Lt Col.^o Leave for two or three Days absents as well as for his Direct Breach of his Orders Given Out the 19th of July 1778—The Coart is of the Oppinion That he is Guilty of the first and Second act of the Charge Exhibited against him and Do therefore Judge him to be Repremanded by his Commanding officer at the Head of the Reg.^t it further appears to the Court the prisioner is not Guilty of the 3 and Last Part of the Charge and do therefore Acquite him. John Summerten Martyrs in Capt. Richfords Camp.^y of the Royall artillery. Tryed for Disserting from his post and taking away with him one of his Majestys Horses is found Guilty and Sentancd to Suffer Death. Joseph Calvert Serg.^t James Mason Corp.^l George Howell & Thomas Corner Private Soldier in the Kings [Orange] Rangers Tryed for Disserting from board the Ship King George being Guard at Harlom where Sergt Culvan Then Commanded the Guard and by force of arms Carrying a Boat from Along Side—the Coart is Oppinion that the prisioner Joseph Calvert Sergt. James Mason Corpl. George Howell & Thomas Corner Private Soldiers are Guilty of the Crimes Laid to thier Charge and Do therefore Sentence the prisioner Joseph Calvert—James Mason and Thomas Corner to Suffer Death and the prisioner George Howell to Receive 1000 Lashes—the Commander in Chief approves of the Above Sentances—

All

All men Actually Invelleaded by the Different Hospittals Boards are to be held in Readiness to Embark
for Europe on the Shortest Notice—and a Return of
all Such men in each Reg.^{t} is to be Sent to the Adj.^{t}
Gen.^{ls} Office by monday Next 24th Instant. An Hospittal Board will Assemble at the Genl. Hospittal on
Friday Next the 13th Instant at 10 OClock in the fore-
noon for the Inspection of Such men as are Considered
unf.^{t} for Further Service and who are not allready In-
villeded. A Packett will Dispatched for Britian in 3
Days here all Letters to be Sent to the Town Majors
Quar.^{s} by Sunday Evening Next—

N. B. All Returns and States of the Provincial
Corps are to be sent to the Inspecter Genl and not
Thier Office for the future   The Sentances by the Genl
Court Martial upon the following Prisioners are to be
put in Execution at the Discreation of Thier Officers
Commanding the Corps to which they belong Viz.
Reg.^{t} Sentances.

    Richard Jasper Pensilvaney Loyalists . 1000 Lashs
    Stephen Beachem 500
    Francis Bouchet 2^d B.^{n} Duly.^{s} 500
    John Gosan   D.^{o} 500
    Calib Boyle 2^d B Jersey V. 500
    Wm. Warden   D.^{o} 500
    Peter Brown M L 500
    George Howell Rangers 1000

The followers of the army under Sentances are to be
punished by The provost Martial.

CAMP FLUSHING FLY 13TH SEPT 78.

Parole,   C Sign.

Field Officer for Duty to Morrow L.t Col.o Chalmers
adj.t M Loyalists Gen.l Dulanceys G.d L A Reg.t pro-
vost G.d R C Vollinteers Orderly Serg.t L A Reg.t A
Corp.l & 4 from the 1st and 3d Batt.n Dulanceys & R
C Vollinteers to mount Daly at the Widow Graunts
House to protect her Property for this Duty to Day
1st Batt.n to Morrow the 3d D.o The Quar.r M.r Gen.l
will find the Most Conveniantest Ground Near the
Encampment of the M: L: to Encamp the Loyal A
M Reg.t in Order to thier being a nearer Compact [?]
Situation with the Other Corps the Ground to be
shown to the Commanding Officer of the Reg.t as Soon
as Possable who will Remove and Incamp there Immediately Frunting East.

R. O. For the Day to Morrow Cap.t Frisby Pickett
and Q.r G.d to morrow L.t Ingils.

No Bows or Trees to be Cut Down on Any account

CAMP FLUSHING FLY SEPT 14TH, 1778.

Field Officer for Duty to Morrow Major Lynch
Adj.t R C Vollinteers Brig.dr Gen.l Dulanceys G.d M L
Provost G.d L. A. Reg.t Guard at Mrs. Grants R C Vo.
Orderly Serg.t M Loyalists.

R. O. For the Day to morrow Cap.t Coston Pickett
& Q.r G.d En.s Bowles. A Return of articles Wanting
to

to Compleat the Drums of the M. L. Sept. 14th, Cap.ᵗ
G. Dulaneys Company a Drum and A Carriage Cap.ᵗ
Jones One Drum head Cap.ᵗ Coston one Drum head
and Sticks. Cap.ᵗ Frisbys a new drum and sticks Capt.
Kennedys a Drum Head and Carriage & Cords It is
Ordered that the Above Artickels may be Immediately
furnished by the Respective Companys of the Batt.ⁿ

HEAD QUARS. NEW YORK SEP.ᵀ 14ᵀᴴ.

All such Officers as have the Commander in Chiefs
Permission to go to Europe are to Send in thier Names
to the Q.ʳ M.ʳ Gen.ˡˢ Office The 17th Instant that A
proper Arrangement may be made for Thier Imbarka-
tion.

CAMP FLUSHING FLY. SEPT. 15TH, 78.

Parole,   C Sign.

Field Officer for Duty to morrow L.ᵗ Col.º Clifton
adg.ᵗ 1ˢᵗ Batt.ⁿ Dulanceys Gen.ˡ Dulanceys G.ᵈ D.º provost G.ᵈ 3ᵈ B. D.º G.ᵈ at Mrs. Graunts 1ˢᵗ B. D.º Orderly Sergt. R C Vollinteer.

R. O. For the Day to morrow Cap.ᵗ Kennedy
pickett and Q.ʳ G.ᵈ to morrow L.ᵗ Parker.

MEMᴰᴹ

Strayed from A Field adjoining Major Wallers
Quar.ˢ a Bay horse about 16 Hands high with a Long
Tayl and a Small mair with a Flaxen main and Tayl
about

about 14 Hands high any soldier who Brings them to Major Waller will be Hansomely Rewarded.

Mem^{DM}

A Red Pockett Book Lost Between the Incampment of the M Loyalists and G^l Dulanceys Q^{rs} Containing only papers that Can be of no use to no one but the Owner—who Ever Brings the Above Book to Capt Key of the M Loyalists will Receive one Guinney Reward and no Questi^{ns} Asked.

Head Quar^s Flushing Fly Sep^t 16th, 1778.

P   C Sign.

Field Officer for Duty to Morrow Major Mc Daniald Adjt. 3^d B. Dulancys G^d at Genl Dulancys 3^d Battⁿ D^o provost G^d D^o M Loyalists and at Mrs. Grants 1st Battⁿ Dulanceys Orderly Serg^t 1st Battⁿ D^o

R. O. For the Day to morrow Capt. Wal^r Dulaney for the Pickett and Q^r Guard to morr^w En^s Monrow.

When any Orders Relative to the men are Isued the Officer to Communicate them them to Every man of their Comp^y Perticulerly to thier Serg^{ts} .

Head Quars. New York Sept. 16th.
Orders.

The Flank Companys of the 10th, 44th, & 52^d are to Join thier Respective Reg^{ts} as soon as Convenient in Order

Order to thier being Drafted into Other Corps Each
Reg^t. of Brittish to Send to thier Adj^t. Gen^{ls} Office by
fryday Next A List of thier men who Have Named
for Garrison Duty by thier Different Hospittal Boords.

Mem.^{DM}

All persons not belonging to the Armey who have
permission to go Europe are to give in thier names to
the Town Major who will make Applycations to the
Q^r. M^r. Gen^{ls} Office For thier Passage.

CAMP FLUSHING FLY. SEP^T 17TH,

Parrole,   C Sign.

Field Officer for Duty to mor^w L^t. Colo. Cruger
Adj^t. L: A. Regt. Genl. Dulanceys Q^{rs} D^o L Provest
G^d 1st Batt^n Dulanceys G^d at Mrs Grants R: C. Vol-
linteer Orderly Serg^t. 3^d Batt^n Dulanceys.

R. O   For the Day to morrow Capt. Frisby pickett
and Q^r. G^d. Lieu^t. Townsand.

CAMP FLUSHING FLY SEPT. 18TH 1778.

Parole.   C Sign.

Field Officer for Duty to mor^w Major Green Adj^t
M: Loyalists Genl. Dulanceys Guard M: Loy^{ts} G^d at
Mrs. Grants 1st Battn. Dulanceys Orderly Serg^t. L:
A: Reg^{ts}.

R. O.   For the Day to morrow Capt. Coston Pickt
and

and Q.^r Guard En.^s Jones Regemtl Coart Martial to set to morrow morning at 9 o Clock. Capt Frisby Prisident.

$$\left.\begin{array}{l} \text{L.}^t \text{ Ingils,} \\ \text{En.}^s \text{ Bowls,} \end{array}\right\} \text{ Members. } \left\{\begin{array}{l} \text{L.}^t \text{ Parker,} \\ \text{En.}^s \text{ Monrow.} \end{array}\right.$$

CAMP FLUSHING FLY. SEPT. 19TH.

Parole,   C Sign.

Field Officer Major Barcly adj.^t 1st Batt Dulanceys Genl Guard D.^o Orderly Serg.^t M Loyalists

The Field Off.^rs when they obtain Leave of Absence are to Acq.^t Major Brig.^de Waller there with thier Returns to Camp all is be anounced. N: B. the Same Rule to be observed in Case of Sickness or any other Henderance from Duty.

R. O: For The Day to morrow C. W. Dulany Pickett & Q.^r G.^d to m.^w Lt Townsand.

CAMP FLUSHING FLY SEPT 20TH, 1778.

Parole,   C Sign.

Field Officer for Duty to m.^w Lt Col.^o Chalmers adj.^t 3^d Batt.^n Dulanceys. Gen.^ls Guard L: A. Reg.^t Guard at Mrs. Grants 1st Dulan.^ys Orderly Serg.^t D.^o.

R. O. For the Day to Morrw. Capt Kennedy pickett & Q.^r G.^d Lt Ingils.

HEAD QUAR^S NEW YORK SEP^{TR} 20TH,

ORDERS.

The Commander in Chief has been Pleased to make the following permotions 9th Reg^t Capt Neal McLain to be Capt Vice Montgumrey Disseas^d 11th July 1778. Lieu^t John Smyth to be Capt Vice McLain permotd D^o 45th Reg^t Major Night Removed from the 35th Reg^t to be Major Vice Saxton Disseased the Majority of the 35th Reg^t to be Sold at the Regulated Price.—for the Bennif^t of Major Saxtons fammely in Consequence of an Order from his Majesty. 62^d Reg^t Capt Lieu^t King Herrington to be Capt Vice Cammell Promoted 18th of Augt 1778—Lieut. George Valaney to be Capt Lieu^t Vice Herrington permoted 18th aug^t. The Cammander in Chief is pleas^d to Order the private men fitt for Service into the 10th, 45th, 52^d to Incorperate in to the 4th, 5th, 27th, 28th, 35th, 40th, 56th, 49th & 55th, Reg^{ts} on Thursday 24th Instant.

The Provision Act^s of those men are to be Immediately Settled to the 24th Instant and thier Other Act^s are to be made up to the 22th of October Next. Incluseff as Soon as the Draughft is made the Commanding Officers of the Reg^{ts} that Receive them will apply for his Majestys Bounty of one Guinny and 1½ P^r man and Give the useual Sertifficates and Creaditt at the Rate of 5 Pound Sterling per man. Prisioners of War Invelieds and men Returned fitt for Garrison Duty

Duty by the Severrall Hospittal Boards are to Ex-
cluded in thier Drafts.

The Genl Court Martial of which Lt Col^o M^{c}pher-
son is Prisident is to Assemble at Brookline to morrow Morning at 10: To perseed in the tryal of all
Such prisioners as shall be Braught before them

HEAD Q^{RS} FLUSHING FLY. SEP^T 21ST, 1778.

Parole   C Sign.

Field Officer for Duty to morrow Major McDaniald
adj^t L. A. Reg^t Brig^{dr} Genl Dulanceys G^d M. L. G^d
at Mrs Graunts 3^d Batt^n Dulanceys Orderly Serg^t D^o.

R. O. For the Day to Morrow Capt Frisby Pickett
and Q^r G^d to Morrow En^s Bowles.

CAMP FLUSHING FLY SEP^T 22^D 78.

Parole,   C Sign.

Field Officer for Duty to morr^w Lt Col^o Cruger
Adj^t M. L. Gen^{ls} G^d 3^d Batt^n Dulanceys G^d at M^{rs}
Graunts 1st B^n D^o Orderly Serg^t L. A. Reg^t

R. O. For the Day to morrow Capt Coston pickett
and Q^r Guard Lt Parker.

HEAD QUAR^S FLUSHING FLY SEP^T 23^D 78.

Parole,   C Sign.

Field Officer for Duty to Morr^w Major Green Adj^t
         1st.

1st Battⁿ Dul. Genl Guard D^o G^d at Mrs. Graunts 3^d Battⁿ D^o Orderly Sergt. M. L.

R. O. For the Day to morr^w Capt Kennedy Pickett and Q^r G^d En^s Monrow—it is again Possitefly Ordered That No Wood is Cutt or fences Destroyed on any Pertenc what ever or any other Injury Done to the Property of Late widdow Waters in the Rare and Left of the Incampment.

HEAD QUARS. NEW YORK SEP^T 24.

A Genl Court Martial Consisting of 3 Field Officers 6 Capt^{ns} & 4 L^t from the 10th, 45th, & 52^d Regt. is to assamble at the City Hall in New York on Saterday Next the 26th Instant at 10 in the fore noon For the Trial of all Such prisioners as Shall be Braught Before them.

Lt Col^o French is Prisident.

	c.	s.
the 10th Regt.	2	1.
45th D^o	2	2.
52^d D^o	2	1.
	6	4.

Capt Adie judge Advocate. En^s Crackitt having Obtaned the Commander in Chiefs Permission to Dispose of his Ensignsy in the 17th Regt. of Foot which he Purchesed. A Blank Commission to Made out Vice Crackit Permoted 10th Sep^t 78

Memorandom.

The Loyal A. Reg^t to Relave the Corpral & 3 from the M: Loyalists at Flushing.

R. O. For the Day to morrow Capt Frisby Pickett & Q^r Guard En^s Jones.

A Reg^{tl} Court Martial to set to Morrow morning at 9 O'Clock

Capt. Kennedy Prisident.

$$\left.\begin{array}{l} \text{En}^s \text{ Jones,} \\ \text{L}^t \text{ Ingils,} \end{array}\right\} \text{Members.} \left\{\begin{array}{l} \text{L}^t \text{ Townsand,} \\ \text{En}^s \text{ Monrow.} \end{array}\right.$$

Lt Sterling & Serg^t Dimant to hold them Selves in Readiness to go to New York on the Recruiting Service in Order to pick up any Straggler from the Regt. that may be Thare.

After Orders.

The Orders of the March of the L: A: Regt. is Counter Manded.

The 3^d Batt^n of Brig^{dr} Genl Dulancys Brig^{de} to hold them Selves in Readiness in thier stead to March to Floyds Neck.

———————

Head Quars. Flushing Fly Sep^t 25TH, 78.

Field Officer for Duty to morrow Major Barckly Adj^t M: Loyalists Genl G D^o Guard at Mrs Grants 1st Batt^n Dulanceys Orderly Serg^t L. A. Regt. The 3^d Batt^n Dulancys to March on Sundy morning to Floyds Neck in Order to Releave the Detatchment of

P.

P. W. A. Vollin^rs and L: A: Regt. on Duty on that Poasts.

HEAD QUAR^S NEW YORK SEP^T 25TH, 1778.

The Offir^s and Non-Commission^d Officers of the 10th, 45th, Reg^ts are to hold them Selves in Readiness to Embark for Europe by the first Oppertunety Thier Camp Aquipage to be Returned to Qu^r Mr Genl Store Upon the useuall Respects as Soon as all thier Draufts are Delivered up The Officers to Apply to Barrick Master to Provide their Quar^s till they Embark.

The Commander in Chiefe is pleased to Make the Following permotions 43^d Reg^t. En^s David Roberts from the 38th Reg^t. to be Lieu^t by Purchase Vice Townsand Prefered 11th Augst. 1778.

HEAD QUAR^S FLUSHING FLY SEPT 26TH.

Field Officer for Duty to Morrow Major McDoniald Adj^t 1st Batt^n Dulancys Genl G^d Loyal A. Regt. G^d at Mrs. Grants 1st Batt^n Dulancys Orderly Sergt. M: Loyalists. The Serg^t and 5 Privates from the 3^d Batt^n Dulancys who have Part of the Guard Over the two Field Peices to be Immediately Releaved by an Eaqual number. R. O. For the Day to morrow Capt. Coston Pickett and Quarter Guard Lt Townsand. A Field Day to Morrow Morning at 7 OClock No man to Absent.

CAMP FLUSHING FLY 27ᵀᴴ SEPᵀ 78.*

Field Offᵗ for Duty to morrow Lᵗ Colᵒ Cruger
Adjᵗ L. A. Regt. Genˡˢ Guard 1ˢᵗ Battⁿ Delancys
Orderly Sergeant Dᵒ

R. O. For the Day to morrow Capt. Kenedy
Picket and Qʳ Guard Lieut Inglis.

HEAD QUARTERS FLUSHING FLEY SEPᵀ 28ᵀᴴ, 1778.

Field Officer for dutay to Morrow Maiger Green
Adgᵗ M Loayls Genarals Guard L A Regᵗ Orderly
Sarjant Dᵒ the Commanding Officers of Corps is to
Bee Anserable that the Soalgers under there Cummond
Dou not Cut Down Trees or destroy fences the Dead
and Brush Wood to be Used for fuel and the Other
Necessary purposes for the Campe.

R. O. For the Day to Morrow Capᵗ W. Dulaney
pichet and Quarter Guard Ensign Boles A Return
from Each Componey of the Men's beeing Cleard off
to the 24 of Augᵗ Inclusive agreeable to former Order
to be Given as Sune Aas Possible.

* * *

CAMP FLUSHING FLY SEPTᴿ 29ᵀᴴ 1778.

Parole,   C Sign.

Field Officer for Duty to morrow Major Barcly

---

*The portion between the asterisks is not in Captain Jones hand-writing.

Adjt.

Adj^t 1st Battⁿ Dulanys Genl Guard M: Loyalists. Orderly Serg^t D^o

R. O. For they Day to morrow Capt. Frisby Pickett and Quar^r Guard Lt Parker.

HEAD QUARS. FLUSHING FLY. SEP^T 30TH.

Parole,   C Sign.

Field Officer for Duty to Morrow Lt Col^o Chalmers adj^t. L. A: Reg^t Gen^{ls} Guard and Orderly Serg^t. 1st Battⁿ Dulancys.

A Court Martial of the Line to Assemble to Morrow Morning at 10 oClock for the Tryal of all Such Prisoners as Braught Before them

Prisident from the 1st Battⁿ Dulancys

Subaltons.

1st Battⁿ Dull^{ys} 1
L : A. Regt 2
M. Loyalists . . . . 1 Members.
                                    ——
Total 4

The Prisioners to have Notice and the Evidances to attend.

R. O. For the Day to Morrow Capt. Coston Pickett and Q^r Guard En^s Monrow.

A Court Martial of the Line attend to Morrow morning Lt Parker.

CAMPE FLUSHING FLY OCTOBER 1ST, 1778.

Parole,   C S

Field officer for Dutay to Morrow Maige McDannel Adgnt M: Loyalst G. Guard and orderly Saejant L. Amerⁿ Rigt.

R O   For the Day to morrow Capt. Kannaday Picket and Quarter Guard Lieu^t Starling.*

HEAD QUAR^S CAMP FLUSHING FLY OCT. 2^D, 1778.

Parole,   C S.

Field Officer for Duty to Morrow Lt. Colo. Cruger adj^t 1st Battⁿ Delancys Gen^{ls} Guard & Orderly Serg^t M. Loyalists.

R. O. For the Day to morrow Capt W. Dulany Pickett & Quarter Guard En^s Jones.

HEAD QUAR^S CAMP FLUSHING FLY OCT^R 3^D, 1778.

Field Officer for Duty to Morrow Major Green Adj^t 1st Battⁿ Delancys Gen^{ls} Guard & Orderly Serg^t D^o

R. O. The Articles of war to be Read to the Men by thier own Off^{rs} to Morrow Morning No Man to take Arms out of the Bell Tent from Evening Roal Calling to Revellee Beating The Offic^r of Companys to Call the Tents Roals at 9: OClock at Night and

---

* This day's entry is not in Captain Jones' handwriting.

Report

Report to the Capt of the Day Such men as may be Abs^t. The Capt of the Day at the Same Time to give the Sentrys Strict Orders to Suffer no non Commissioned Offi^r or Soldier to Pass them from Camp Untill he Gives his further Orders In the Morning Such as attempt it to be made prisioners.

Lieu^t. Sterling to Return to Capt. Frisbys Company to do Duty For the Day to Morrow Capt Frisby Picket This Evening Lt Townsand Pickett & Quart^r Guard to Morrow.

———

Morning Orders 4th Oct. 78.

A Reg^{tl} Court Martial to set at 9 O'Clock.

Capt. Jones. Presidt.

En^s Cannon ⎱ Members ⎰ L^t. Townsend
Lieu^t. Sterling, ⎰ ⎱ En^s. Bowles.

———

CAMP FLUSHING FLY 4 OCTR. 178.

Field Officer for Duty to Morr^w Major Barclay Adj^t. L. A. Reg^t. Gen^{ls} Guard and Orderly Serg^t L: A: Regt.

R. O. For the Day to Morrow Capt. Kennedy Qr. Guard En^s. Cannon Picket this Evening L^t. Ingils.

———

HEAD QUAR^s CAMP FLUSHING FLY OCT^R 5, 1778.

Field Officer for Duty to Morrow L^t. Colo. Chalmers adj^t. M : Loyalists Gen^{ls} Guard & Orderly Serg^t D^o The Troops to Beat at 9 OClock till further Orders.

R. O.

R. O   For the Day to morrow Capt Jones Q.^r G.^d En.^s Cannon Pickett Lt Sinclier.

HEAD QUAR.^S NEW YORK. OCT. 5TH, 78.

A Subaltons Guard from B. Genl Delancys Brigade to be furnished for the protection of the Wood Cutters on Long Island Upon Applycation from Lieut. Waugh* or Eaither of the Barrick Masters Deputies and the Commd.^r in Chiefs Trusts that the Off.^s Commanding that Brigade will give every Necessary assistance for Carrying on that Service.

HEAD QUAR.^S FLUSHING FLY OCT.^R 6TH, 1778.

Field Off.^r for Duty to morrow Major McDanald Adj.^t Gen.^{ls} Guard and Orderly Serj.^t 1st Batt.ⁿ Delancy.

Reg.^{tl} Orders.

A Serj.^t or Corp.^l of each Company to Parade the Men for Guard of theire Respective Companys an hour before Guard Manting and see that they are properly Dressd & Clean.   Whatever Serg.^t or Corporal Parade a Man Improperly Dress.^d will be Confined for Disobediance of Orders—

For the Day to morrow Capt W. Dulany for Guard En.^s Bowles Pickett Lt Parker.

------

* See *Rivington* for Sept. 9, 1778.

Morning

Morning Orders 7ᵗʰ Octᵣ 7 OClock.

In Consiquence of the Orders from the Inspecter Genˡ Office New York two Detatchments of a Sergᵗ 12 Rank & file each are to March Immediately. one to harlem as a Guard to the Genˡ Hospittal in that Place. & the Other to go On Boord the Kings George Laying in Creek. 1ˢᵗ Battⁿ Delancys Takes the Hospittal Guard the M : Loyalists the Ship Guard.

HEAD QUARS. FLUSHING FLY OCTR. 7TH, 1778.

Parole,   C Sign.

Field Officer for Duty to Morrow Colᵒ Cruger Adjᵗ Genˡ Guard and Orderly L. A : Regt. R. O. For the Day to morrow Capᵗ Key Qᵣ Gᵈ Lᵗ Parker Pickett Enˢ Monrow.

CAMP FLUSHING FLY OCTᴿ 8TH, 78.

Field Officer for Duty to morrow Major Green Adlᵗ &Genˡˢ Gard and Orderly Sergᵗ M Loyalists.

R. O. For the Day to morrow Capt. Coston Qᵣ Guard Lᵗ Sterling Pickett Enˢ Jones.

A Regᵗˡ Court Martial to set to morrow Morning at 10 O'Clock

Capt. W. Dulany Presᵈᵗ

Enˢ Sterling, ⎫ Members.⎰ Lᵗ Sterling,
Lieuᵗ Parker, ⎭   ⎱ Enˢ Bowles.

HEAD QUARS FLUSHING FLY OCT^R 9TH 1778.

Field Officer for Duty to Morrow Major Barcly Adj^t. Genl. Guard and Orderly Serg^t. M: Loyalists. Each Reg^ts to Construct Proper Kitchens or Cooking Plac^s and No Soldier Suffered to Cook from them which the Visseting Officer will be Cearefull to see Executed.

R. O. For the Day to Morrow Capt. G. Dulany Q^r. G^d Ens Jones Pickett L^t. Townsand.

HEAD QUARS CAMP FLUSHING FLY 10TH OCT^R 78.

Parole, *Nix.*   C Sign, *Less.*

Field Officer for Duty to morrow L^t. Col^o Chalmers Adj^t. Gen^ls Guard and Orderly Serg^t. 1st Batt^n Dulancys.

Regem^tl Orders.

For the Day to Morrow Capt. Kennedy Q^r. Guard for Pickett

HEAD QUAR^s FLUSHING FLY OCT^R 11TH 1778.

Field Officer for Duty to Morrow Major McDaniald Adj^t. Genr^ls Guard and Orderly Sergeant L. A. Regement.

R. O. For the Day to Morrow Capt. Jones Quarter Guard Lieu^t. Ingils for Pickett L^t. Sinclier.

HEAD QUARS. FLUSHING FLY OCT.^R 12TH, 1778.

Field Officer for Duty to Morrow Col.º Cruger Adj.^t Gena^{ls} Guard and Orderly Serg.^t 1st Battⁿ Dulancys

A More Punctial Obediance of Orders of the 17th Sep.^t 78. is Expected Relative to the Leave of the Field Officers Their henderance from Duty by sickness or Other ways—which Orders have been Payed Very Little Attention to by some and Totally Disregarded by Others. Such Neglacts and unregularritys will in Futer be taken notice on in a More Perticler manner.

Diserted from the 27th Dragoons a Dragoon with a Black Stallion about 15 hands high with a Regementall Saddle and Bridle of the 17th Dragoons The Holster Cap Made of white Goat Skin & the Dragoon a Short man Marked much with the small Pox. Five Guinneys Reward will be Given by the Paymaster for the Recoverry of the horse besides 40 Shillings for takeing of the Diserter.

R. O. For the Day to Morrow Capt W. Dulany Q.^r Guard En^s Cannon Pickett Lt Sinclier as the Battⁿ is to be Inspected on Wednes Day Morning Early the Capt^{ns} to be Anserable that thier Companys Make a Clean and Uniform Appearance and that thier Make no fires in Thier Tents.

*   *   *   *   *   *   *   *   *

th^s Books Orders Out Last Octr. 12th, 1778.

Capt Calib Jones his Orderly Book September 11, 1778.

god

god gives him grace therein to book[?] and not to Look But to under stand that Learning is better than house and Land.

Zacriah Baley Sargant

James Love Sargant

Joshua Merrill Sargant

John White Corpal

Jacob Rodgers Corpral

Obediah Smith

Learning proves most Exolent

when house and land is gone and Spent.

Head Quarters Camp Flush-
ing Fly Septr.
30th 1778

www.ingramcontent.com/pod-product-compliance
Lightning Source LLC
Chambersburg PA
CBHW072205270326
41930CB00011B/2543